1/92

THE SECOND AMENDMENT

The ★★★ AMERICAN HERITAGE HISTORY *of the* BILL *of* RIGHTS

THE SECOND AMENDMENT

Joan C. Hawxhurst

Introduction by
WARREN E. BURGER
Chief Justice of the United States
1969–1986

Silver Burdett Press

This book is dedicated to Steve, my staff and my shelter, as together we begin our climb to the top of the mountain.

Cover: The National Guard. One of the controversies that swirls around the Second Amendment is whether the right to keep and bear arms is a right of the community related to service in the militia or an individual right or both.

CONSULTANTS:

Elizabeth Blackmar
Assistant Professor of History
Columbia College
New York, New York

Frank de Varona
Associate Superintendent
Dade County Public Schools
Miami, Florida

Text and Cover Design: Circa 86, Inc.

Copyright © 1991 by Gallin House Press, Inc.
Introduction copyright © 1991 by Silver Burdett Press, Inc.

Published by Silver Burdett Press, Inc., a division of Simon & Schuster, Inc., Englewood Cliffs, N.J. 07632.

Library of Congress Cataloging-in-Publication Data

Hawxhurst, Joan C.
   The Second Amendment/by Joan C. Hawxhurst: with an introduction
by Warren E. Burger.
   p. cm.—(The American heritage history of the Bill of
Rights)
   Includes bibliographical references and indexes.
   Summary: Traces the historical origins of provisions of the Second Amendment: the right to keep and bear arms, and the maintenance of a militia.
   1. United States—Constitutional law—Amendments—2nd—History—
Juvenile literature. 2. Firearms—Law and legislation—United
States—History—Juvenile literature. 3. United States—Militia—
History—Juvenile literature. [1. United States—Constitutional
law—Amendments—2nd—History. 2. Firearms—Law and legislation—
History. 3. United States—Militia—History.] I. Title.
II. Series.
KF4558 2nd. H39 1991
344. 73'0533—dc20
[347.304533]   90-19300
                                                                                      CIP
                                                                                      AC

Manufactured in the United States of America.

ISBN 0-382-24180-0 [lib. bdg.]
10 9 8 7 6 5 4 3 2 1

ISBN 0-382-24193-2 [pbk.]
10 9 8 7 6 5 4 3 2 1

ONTENTS

INTRODUCTION

WARREN E. BURGER
Chief Justice of the United States, 1969–1986

The Second Amendment gave the American people "the right . . . to keep and bear Arms." Since there was no national army when the amendment was written, it justifies itself on the basis of national security: "A well regulated Militia being necessary to the security of a free State." The amendment grew out of the deep-seated fear of a "national" or "standing" army, as shown in the 1789 debate in Congress on James Madison's proposed Bill of Rights. In that debate Elbridge Gerry gave voice to these concerns, arguing that a state militia was necessary "to prevent the establishment of a standing army,' the bane of liberty. . . . Whenever governments mean to invade the rights and liberties of the people, they always attempt to destroy the militia in order to raise an army upon their ruins." If the state "militia" was to be "well regulated," it follows that all use of arms may be regulated by law.

Concepts of liberty—the values liberty protects—inspired the Framers of our Constitution and the Bill of Rights to some of their most impassioned eloquence. "Liberty, the greatest of earthly possessions—give us that precious jewel, and you may take everything else," declaimed Patrick Henry. Those toilers in the "vineyard of liberty" sensed the historic nature of their mission, and their foresight accounts for the survival of the Bill of Rights.

Today, citizens continue to exercise their Second Amendment rights by serving in the military—the National Guard and the armed services. All Americans owe these active service people our gratitude.

But the application of the Second Amendment to the civilian population is extremely controversial because it is at the center of the gun control issue. Citizens must consider that the right to bear arms may be abused—that it may be used in criminal activities to the detriment of us all. Citizens and their lawmaking delegates must decide whether the regulation of firearms should be susceptible to an equal amount of regulation as, say, driving a car. Because our metropolitan centers are setting new records for homicides by handguns and machine guns, people must decide whether the purchase of such weapons should be "well regulated" to ensure the "domestic tranquillity" promised in the Constitution.

The long-term success of the system of ordered liberty set up by our Constitution was by no means foreordained. The bicentennial of the

Bill of Rights provides an opportunity to reflect on the significance of the freedoms we enjoy and to commit ourselves to exercise the civic responsibilities required to sustain our constitutional system. The Constitution, including its first ten amendments, the Bill of Rights, has survived two centuries because of its unprecedented philosophical premise: that it derives its power from the people. It is not a grant from the government to the people. In 1787 the masters—the people—were saying to their government—their servant—that certain rights are inherent, natural rights and that they belong to the people, who had those rights before any governments existed. The function of government, they said, was to protect these rights.

The Bill of Rights also owes its continued vitality to the fact that it was drafted by experienced, practical politicians. It was a product of the Framers' essential mistrust of the frailties of human nature. This led them to develop the idea of the separation of powers and to make the Bill of Rights part of the permanent Constitution.

Moreover, the document was designed to be flexible, and the role of providing that flexibility through interpretation has fallen to the judiciary. Indeed, the first commander in chief, George Washington, gave the Supreme Court its moral marching orders two centuries ago when he said, "the administration of justice is the firmest pillar of government." The principle of judicial review as a check on government has perhaps nowhere been more significant than in the protection of individual liberties. It has been my privilege, along with my colleagues on the Court, to ensure the continued vitality of our Bill of Rights. As John Marshall asked, long before he became chief justice, "To what quarter will you look for a protection from an infringement on the Constitution, if you will not give the power to the judiciary?"

But the preservation of the Bill of Rights is not the sole responsibility of the judiciary. Rather, judges, legislatures, and presidents are partners with every American; liberty is the responsibility of every public officer and every citizen. In this spirit all Americans should become acquainted with the principles and history of this most remarkable document. Its bicentennial should not be simply a celebration but the beginning of an ongoing process. Americans must—by their conduct—guarantee that it continues to protect the rights of our uniquely multicultural population. We must not fail to exercise our rights to vote, to participate in government and community activities, and to implement the principles of liberty, tolerance, and justice for all.

THE AMERICAN HERITAGE
HISTORY OF THE BILL OF RIGHTS

THE FIRST AMENDMENT
by Philip A. Klinkner

THE SECOND AMENDMENT
by Joan C. Hawxhurst

THE THIRD AMENDMENT
by Burnham Holmes

THE FOURTH AMENDMENT
by Paula A. Franklin

THE FIFTH AMENDMENT
by Burnham Holmes

THE SIXTH AMENDMENT
by Eden Force

THE SEVENTH AMENDMENT
by Lila E. Summer

THE EIGHTH AMENDMENT
by Vincent Buranelli

THE NINTH AMENDMENT
by Philip A. Klinkner

THE TENTH AMENDMENT
by Judith Adams

The Bill of Rights

AMENDMENT 1*

Article Congress shall make no law respecting an establishment of religion, or prohibiting the free exercise thereof; or abridging the freedom of speech, or of the press; or the right of the people peaceably to assemble, and to petition the Government for a redress of grievances.

AMENDMENT 2

Article A well regulated Militia, being necessary to the security of a free State, the right of the people to keep and bear Arms, shall not be infringed.

AMENDMENT 3

Article No Soldier shall, in time of peace be quartered in any house, without the consent of the Owner, nor in time of war, but in a manner to be prescribed by law.

AMENDMENT 4

Article The right of the people to be secure in their persons, houses, papers, and effects, against unreasonable searches and seizures, shall not be violated, and no Warrants shall issue, but upon probable cause, supported by Oath or affirmation, and particularly describing the place to be searched, and the persons or things to be seized.

AMENDMENT 5

Article No person shall be held to answer for a capital, or otherwise infamous crime, unless on a presentment or indictment of a Grand Jury, except in cases arising in the land or naval forces, or in the Militia, when in actual service in time of War or public danger; nor shall any person be subject for the same offence to be twice put in jeopardy of life or limb; nor shall be compelled in any criminal case to be a witness against himself, nor be deprived of life, liberty, or property, without due process of law; nor shall private property be taken for public use without just compensation.

AMENDMENT 6

Article In all criminal prosecutions, the accused shall enjoy the right to a speedy and public trial, by an impartial jury of the State and district wherein the crime shall have been committed, which district shall have been previously ascertained by law, and to be informed of the nature and cause of the accusation; to be confronted with the witnesses against him; to have compulsory process for obtaining Witnesses in his favor, and to have the assistance of counsel for his defence.

AMENDMENT 7

Article In Suits at common law, where the value in controversy shall exceed twenty dollars, the right of trial by jury shall be preserved, and no fact tried by a jury, shall be otherwise reexamined in any Court of the United States, than according to the rules of the common law.

AMENDMENT 8

Article Excessive bail shall not be required, nor excessive fines imposed, nor cruel and unusual punishments inflicted.

AMENDMENT 9

Article The enumeration in the Constitution, of certain rights, shall not be construed to deny or disparage others retained by the people.

AMENDMENT 10

Article The powers not delegated to the United States by the Constitution, nor prohibited by it to the States, are reserved to the States respectively, or to the people.

*Note that each of the first ten amendments to the original Constitution is called an "Article." None of these amendments had actual numbers at the time of their ratification.

TIME CHART

THE HISTORY OF THE
BILL OF RIGHTS

1770s–1790s

1774 Quartering Act
1775 Revolutionary War begins
1776 Declaration of Independence is signed.
1783 Revolutionary War ends.
1787 Constitutional Convention writes the U.S. Constitution.
1788 U.S. Constitution is ratified by most states.
1789 Congress proposes the Bill of Rights
1791 The Bill of Rights is ratified by the states.
1792 Militia Act

1800s–1820s

1803 *Marbury* v. *Madison.* Supreme Court declares that it has the power of judicial review and exercises it. This is the first case in which the Court holds a law of Congress unconstitutional.
1807 Trial of Aaron Burr. Ruling that juries may have knowledge of a case so long as they have not yet formed an opinion.
1813 Kentucky becomes the first state to outlaw concealed weapons.
1824 *Gibbons* v. *Ogden.* Supreme Court defines Congress's power to regulate commerce, including trade between states and within states if that commerce affects other states.

1830s–1870s

1833 *Barron* v. *Baltimore.* Supreme Court rules that Bill of Rights applies only to actions of the federal government, not to the states and local governments.

1851 *Cooley* v. *Board of Wardens of the Port of Philadelphia.* Supreme Court rules that states can apply their own rules to some foreign and interstate commerce if their rules are of a local nature—unless or until Congress makes rules for particular situations.

1857 *Dred Scott* v. *Sandford.* Supreme Court denies that African Americans are citizens even if they happen to live in a "free state."

1862 Militia Act

1865 Thirteenth Amendment is ratified. Slavery is not allowed in the United States.

1868 Fourteenth Amendment is ratified. All people born or naturalized in the United States are citizens. Their privileges and immunities are protected, as are their life, liberty, and property according to due process. They have equal protection of the laws.

1873 *Slaughterhouse* cases. Supreme Court rules that the Fourteenth Amendment does not limit state power to make laws dealing with economic matters. Court mentions the unenumerated right to political participation.

1876 *United States* v. *Cruikshank.* Supreme Court rules that the right to bear arms for a lawful purpose is not an absolute right granted by the Constitution. States can limit this right and make their own gun-control laws.

1880s–1920s

1884 *Hurtado* v. *California.* Supreme Court rules that the right to a grand jury indictment doesn't apply to the states.

1896 *Plessy* v. *Ferguson.* Supreme Court upholds a state law based on "separate but equal" facilities for different races.

1903 Militia Act creates National Guard.

1905 *Lochner* v. *New York.* Supreme Court strikes down a state law regulating maximum work hours.

1914 *Weeks* v. *United States.* Supreme Court establishes that illegally obtained evidence, obtained by unreasonable search and seizure, cannot be used in federal trials.

1918 *Hammer* v. *Dagenhart.* Supreme Court declares unconstitutional a federal law prohibiting the shipment between states of goods made by young children.

1923 *Meyer* v. *Nebraska.* Supreme Court rules that a law banning teaching of foreign languages or teaching in languages other than English is unconstitutional. Court says that certain areas of people's private lives are protected from government interference.

1925 *Carroll* v. *United States.* Supreme Court allows searches of automobiles without a search warrant under some circumstances.

1925 *Gitlow* v. *New York.* Supreme Court rules that freedom of speech and freedom of the press are protected from state actions by the Fourteenth Amendment.

1930s

1931 *Near* v. *Minnesota*. Supreme Court rules that liberty of the press and of speech are safeguarded from state action.

1931 *Stromberg* v. *California*. Supreme Court extends concept of freedom of speech to symbolic actions such as displaying a flag.

1932 *Powell* v. *Alabama* (*First Scottsboro* case). Supreme Court rules that poor defendants have a right to an appointed lawyer when tried for crimes that may result in the death penalty.

1934 National Firearms Act becomes the first federal law to restrict the keeping and bearing of arms.

1935 *Norris* v. *Alabama* (*Second Scottsboro* case). Supreme Court reverses the conviction of an African American because of the long continued excluding of African Americans from jury service in the trial area.

1937 *Palko* v. *Connecticut*. Supreme Court refuses to require states to protect people under the double jeopardy clause of the Bill of Rights. But the case leads to future application of individual rights in the Bill of Rights to the states on a case-by-case basis.

1937 *DeJonge* v. *Oregon*. Supreme Court rules that freedom of assembly and petition are protected against state laws.

1939 *United States* v. *Miller*. Supreme Court rules that National Firearms Act of 1934 does not violate Second Amendment.

1940s–1950s

1940 *Cantwell* v. *Connecticut*. Supreme Court rules that free exercise of religion is protected against state laws.

1943 *Barnette* v. *West Virginia State Board of Education*. Supreme Court rules that flag salute laws are unconstitutional.

1946 *Theil* v. *Pacific Railroad*. Juries must be a cross section of the community, excluding no group based on religion, race, sex, or economic status.

1947 *Everson* v. *Board of Education*. Supreme Court rules that government attempts to impose religious practices, the establishment of religion, is forbidden to the states.

1948 *In re Oliver*. Supreme Court rules that defendants have a right to public trial in nonfederal trials.

1949 *Wolf* v. *California*. Supreme Court rules that freedom from unreasonable searches and seizures also applies to states.

1954 *Brown* v. *Board of Education of Topeka*. Supreme Court holds that segregation on the basis of race (in public education) denies equal protection of the laws.

1958 *NAACP* v. *Alabama*. Supreme Court rules that the privacy of membership lists in an organization is part of the right to freedom of assembly and association.

1960s

1961 *Mapp* v. *Ohio*. Supreme Court rules that illegally obtained evidence must not be allowed in state criminal trials.

1962 *Engel* v. *Vitale*. Supreme Court strikes down state-sponsored school prayer, saying it is no business of government to compose official prayers as part of a religious program carried on by the government.

1963 *Gideon* v. *Wainwright*. Supreme Court rules that the right of people accused of serious crimes to be represented by an appointed counsel applies to state criminal trials.

1964 Civil Rights Act is passed.

1964 *Malloy* v. *Hogan*. Supreme Court rules that the right to protection against forced self-incrimination applies to state trials.

1965 *Griswold* v. *Connecticut*. Supreme Court rules that there is a right to privacy in marriage and declares unconstitutional a state law banning the use of or the giving of information about birth control.

1965 *Pointer* v. *Texas*. Supreme Court rules that the right to confront witnesses against an accused person applies to state trials.

1966 *Parker* v. *Gladden*. Supreme Court ruling is interpreted to mean that the right to an impartial jury is applied to the states.

1966 *Miranda* v. *Arizona*. Supreme Court extends the protection against forced self-incrimination. Police have to inform people in custody of their rights before questioning them.

1967 *Katz* v. *United States*. Supreme Court rules that people's right to be free of unreasonable searches includes protection against electronic surveillance.

1967 *Washington* v. *Texas*. Supreme Court rules that accused people have the right to have witnesses in their favor brought into court.

1967 *In re Gault*. Supreme Court rules that juvenile proceedings that might lead to the young person's being sent to a state institution must follow due process and fair treatment. These include the rights against forced self-incrimination, to counsel, to confront witnesses.

1967 *Klopfer* v. *North Carolina*. Supreme Court rules that the right to a speedy trial applies to state trials.

1968 *Duncan* v. *Louisiana*. Supreme Court rules that the right to a jury trial in criminal cases applies to state trials.

1969 *Benton* v. *Maryland*. Supreme Court rules that the protection against double jeopardy applies to the states.

1969 *Brandenburg* v. *Ohio*. Supreme Court rules that speech calling for the use of force or crime can only be prohibited if it is directed to bringing about immediate lawless action and is likely to bring about such action.

1970s–1990s

1970 *Williams* v. *Florida*. Juries in cases that do not lead to the possibility of the death penalty may consist of six jurors rather than twelve.

1971 *Pentagon Papers* case. Freedom of the press is protected by forbidding prior restraint.

1971 *Duke Power Co.* v. *Carolina Environmental Study Group, Inc.* Supreme Court upholds state law limiting liability of federally licensed power companies in the event of a nuclear accident.

1972 *Furman* v. *Georgia*. Supreme Court rules that the death penalty (as it was then decided upon) is cruel and unusual punishment and therefore unconstitutional.

1972 *Argersinger* v. *Hamlin*. Supreme Court rules that right to counsel applies to all criminal cases that might involve a jail term.

1973 *Roe* v. *Wade*. Supreme Court declares that the right to privacy protects a woman's right to end pregnancy by abortion under specified circumstances.

1976 *Gregg* v. *Georgia*. Supreme Court rules that the death penalty is to be allowed if it is decided upon in a consistent and reasonable way, if the sentencing follows strict guidelines, and if the penalty is not required for certain crimes.

1976 *National League of Cities* v. *Usery*. Supreme Court holds that the Tenth Amendment prevents Congress from making federal minimum wage and overtime rules apply to state and city workers.

1981 *Quilici* v. *Village of Morton Grove*. U.S. district court upholds a local ban on sale and possession of handguns.

1985 *Garcia* v. *San Antonio Metropolitan Transit Authority*. Supreme Court rules that Congress can make laws dealing with wages and hour rules applied to city-owned transportation systems.

1989 *Webster* v. *Reproductive Health Services.* Supreme Court holds that a state may prohibit all use of public facilities and publicly employed staff in abortions.

1989 *Johnson* v. *Texas*. Supreme Court rules that flag burning is protected and is a form of "symbolic speech."

1990 *Cruzan* v. *Missouri Department of Health*. Supreme Court recognizes for the first time a very sick person's right to die without being forced to undergo unwanted medical treatment and a person's right to a living will.

1990 *Noriega–CNN* case. Supreme Court upholds lower federal court's decision to allow temporary prior restraint thus limiting the First Amendment right of freedom of the press.

The Birth of the Bill of Rights

"We hold these truths to be self-evident, that all men are created equal, that they are endowed by their Creator with certain unalienable Rights, that among these are Life, Liberty, and the pursuit of Happiness."

THE DECLARATION OF INDEPENDENCE (1776)

A brave Chinese student standing in front of a line of tanks, Eastern Europeans marching against the secret police, happy crowds dancing on top of the Berlin Wall—these were recent scenes of people trying to gain their freedom or celebrating it. The scenes and the events that sparked them will live on in history. They also show the lasting gift that is our Bill of Rights. The freedoms guaranteed by the Bill of Rights have guided and inspired millions of people all over the world in their struggle for freedom.

The Colonies Gain Their Freedom

Like many countries today, the United States fought to gain freedom and democracy for itself. The American colonies had a revolution from 1775 to 1783 to free themselves from British rule.

The colonists fought to free themselves because they believed that the British had violated, or gone against, their rights. The colonists held what some considered the extreme idea that all

James Madison is known as both the "Father of the Constitution" and the "Father of the Bill of Rights." In 1789 he proposed to Congress the amendments that became the Bill of Rights. Madison served two terms as president of the United States from 1809 to 1817.

The Raising of the Liberty Pole by John McRae. In 1776, American colonists hoisted liberty poles as symbols of liberty and freedom from British rule. At the top they usually placed a liberty cap. Such caps resembled the caps given to slaves in ancient Rome when they were freed.

persons are born with certain rights. They believed that these rights could not be taken away, even by the government. The importance our nation gave to individual rights can be seen in the Declaration of Independence. The Declaration, written by Thomas Jefferson in 1776, states:

We hold these truths to be self-evident, that all men are created equal, that they are endowed by their Creator with certain unalienable Rights, that among these are Life, Liberty, and the pursuit of Happiness.

The United States won its independence from Britain in 1783. But with freedom came the difficult job of forming a government. The Americans wanted a government that was strong enough to keep peace and prosperity, but not so strong that it might take away the rights for which the Revolution had been fought. The Articles of Confederation was the country's first written plan of government.

The Articles of Confederation, becoming law in 1781, created a weak national government. The defects in the Articles soon became clear to many Americans. Because the United States did not have a strong national government, its economy suffered. Under the Articles, Congress did not have the power to tax. It had to ask the states for money or borrow it. There was no separate president or court system. Nine of the states had to agree before Congress's bills became law. In 1786 economic problems caused farmers in Massachusetts to revolt. The national government was almost powerless to stop the revolt. It was also unable to build an army or navy strong enough to protect the United States's borders and its ships on the high seas.

The Constitution Is Drawn Up

The nation's problems had to be solved. So, in February 1787, the Continental Congress asked the states to send delegates to a convention to discuss ways of improving the Articles. That May, fifty-five delegates, from every state except Rhode Island, met in Philadelphia. The group included some of the country's most famous leaders: George Washington, hero of the Revolution; Benjamin Franklin, publisher, inventor, and diplomat; and James Madison, a leading critic of the Articles. Madison would soon become the guiding force behind the Constitutional Convention.

After a long, hot summer of debate the delegates finally drew up the document that became the U.S. Constitution. It set up a strong central government. But it also divided power between three branches of the federal government. These three branches were the executive branch (the presidency), the legislative branch (Congress), and the judicial branch (the courts). Each was given one part of the government's power. This division was to make sure that no single branch became so powerful that it could violate the people's rights.

The legislative branch (made up of the House of Representatives and the Senate) would have the power to pass laws, raise taxes and spend money, regulate the national economy, and declare war. The executive branch was given the power to carry out the laws, run foreign affairs, and command the military.

The Signing of the Constitution painted by Thomas Rossiter. The Constitutional Convention met in Philadelphia from May into September 1787. The proposed Constitution contained protection for some individual rights such as protection against *ex post facto* laws and bills of attainder. When the Constitution was ratified by the required number of states in 1788, however, it did not have a bill of rights.

The role of the judicial branch in this plan was less clear. The Constitution said that the judicial branch would have "judicial power." However, it was unclear exactly what this power was. Over the years "judicial power" has come to mean "judicial review." The power of judicial review allows the federal courts to reject laws passed by Congress or the state legislatures that they believe violate the Constitution.

Judicial review helps protect our rights. It allows federal courts to reject laws that violate the Constitution's guarantees of individual rights. Because of this power, James Madison believed that the courts would be an "impenetrable bulwark," an unbreakable wall, against any attempt by government to take away these rights.

The Constitution did more than divide the power of the federal government among the three branches. It also divided power between the states and the federal government. This division of power is known as *federalism*. Federalism means that the federal

government has control over certain areas. These include regulating the national economy and running foreign and military affairs. The states have control over most other areas. For example, they regulate their economies and make most other laws. Once again, the Framers (writers) of the Constitution hoped that the division of powers would keep both the states and the federal government from becoming too strong and possibly violating individual rights.

The new Constitution did *not,* however, contain a bill of rights. Such a bill would list the people's rights and would forbid the government from interfering with them. The only discussion of the topic came late in the convention. At that time, George Mason of Virginia called for a bill of rights. A Connecticut delegate, Roger Sherman, disagreed. He claimed that a bill of rights was not needed. In his view, the Constitution did not take away any of the rights in the bills of rights in the state constitutions. These had been put in place during the Revolution. The other delegates agreed with Roger Sherman. Mason's proposal was voted down by all.

Yet the Constitution was not without guarantees of individual rights. One of these rights was the protection of *habeas corpus.* This is a legal term that refers to the right of someone who has been arrested to be brought into court and formally charged with a crime. Another right forbade *ex post facto* laws. These are laws that outlaw actions that took place before the passage of the laws. Other parts of the Constitution forbade bills of attainder (laws pronouncing a person guilty of a crime without trial), required jury trials, restricted convictions for treason, and guaranteed a republican form of government. That is a government in which political power rests with citizens who vote for elected officials and representatives responsible to the voters. The Constitution also forbade making public officials pass any "religious test." This meant that religious requirements could not be forced on public officials.

The Debate Over the New Constitution

Once it was written, the Constitution had to be ratified, or approved, by nine of the states before it could go into effect. The new

Constitution created much controversy. Heated battles raged in many states over whether or not to approve the document. One of the main arguments used by those who opposed the Constitution (the Anti-Federalists) was that the Constitution made the federal government too strong. They feared that it might violate the rights of the people just as the British government had. Although he had helped write the Constitution, Anti-Federalist George Mason opposed it for this reason. He claimed that he would sooner chop off his right hand than put it to the Constitution as it then stood.

To correct what they viewed as flaws in the Constitution, the Anti-Federalists insisted that it have a bill of rights. The fiery orator of the Revolution, Patrick Henry, another Anti-Federalist, exclaimed, "Liberty, the greatest of all earthly blessings—give us that precious jewel, and you may take every thing else!"

Although he was not an Anti-Federalist, Thomas Jefferson also believed that a bill of rights was needed. He wrote a letter to James Madison, a wavering Federalist, in which he said: "A bill of rights is what the people are entitled to against every government on earth."

Supporters of the Constitution (the Federalists) argued that it did not need a bill of rights. One reason they stated, similar to that given at the Philadelphia convention, was that most state constitutions had a bill of rights. Nothing in the Constitution would limit or abolish these rights. In 1788 James Madison wrote that he thought a bill of rights would provide only weak "parchment barriers" against attempts by government to take away individual rights. He believed that history had shown that a bill of rights was ineffective on "those occasions when its control [was] needed most."

The views of the Anti-Federalists seem to have had more support than did those of the Federalists. The Federalists came to realize that without a bill of rights, the states might not approve the new Constitution. To ensure ratification, the Federalists therefore agreed to support adding a bill of rights to the Constitution.

With this compromise, eleven of the thirteen states ratified the Constitution by July 1788. The new government of the United States was born. The two remaining states, North Carolina and

Rhode Island, in time accepted the new Constitution. North Carolina approved it in November 1789 and Rhode Island in May 1790.

James Madison Calls for a Bill of Rights

On April 30, 1789, George Washington took the oath of office as president. The new government was launched. One of its first jobs was to amend, or change, the Constitution to include a bill of rights. This is what many of the states had called for during the ratification process. Leading this effort in the new Congress was James Madison. He was a strong supporter of individual rights. As a member of the Virginia legislature, he had helped frame the Virginia Declaration of Rights. He had also fought for religious liberty.

Madison, however, had at first opposed including a bill of rights. But his views had changed. He feared that the Constitution would not be ratified by enough states to become law unless the Federalists offered to include a bill of rights. Madison also knew that many people were afraid of the new government. He feared they might oppose its actions or attempt to undo it. He said a bill of rights "will kill the opposition everywhere, and by putting an end to disaffection to [discontent with] the Government itself, enable the administration to venture on measures not otherwise safe."

On June 8, 1789, the thirty-eight-year-old Madison rose to speak in the House of Representatives. He called for several changes to the Constitution that contained the basis of our present Bill of Rights. Despite his powerful words, Madison's speech did not excite his listeners. Most Federalists in Congress opposed a bill of rights. Others believed that the new Constitution should be given more time to operate before Congress considered making any changes. Many Anti-Federalists wanted a new constitutional convention. There, they hoped to greatly limit the powers of the federal government. These Anti-Federalists thought that adding a bill of rights to the Constitution would prevent their movement for a new convention.

Finally, in August, Madison persuaded the House to consider

his amendments. The House accepted most of them. However, instead of being placed in the relevant sections of the Constitution, as Madison had called for, the House voted to add them as separate amendments. This change—listing the amendments together—made the Bill of Rights the distinct document that it is today.

After approval by the House, the amendments went to the Senate. The Senate dropped what Madison considered the most important part of his plan. This was the protection of freedom of the press, freedom of religious belief, and the right to trial by jury from violation by the states. Protection of these rights from violation by state governments would have to wait until after the Fourteenth Amendment was adopted in 1868.

The House and the Senate at last agreed on ten amendments to protect individual rights. What rights were protected? Here is a partial list:

The First Amendment protects freedom of religion, of speech, of the press, of peaceful assembly, and of petition.

The Second Amendment gives to the states the right to keep a militia (a volunteer, reserve military force) and to the people the right to keep and bear arms.

The Third Amendment prevents the government from keeping troops in private homes during wartime.

The Fourth Amendment protects individuals from unreasonable searches and seizures by the government.

The Fifth Amendment states that the government must get an indictment (an official ruling that a crime has been committed) before someone can be tried for a serious crime. This amendment bans "double jeopardy." This means trying a person twice for the same criminal offense. It also protects people from having to testify against themselves in court.

The Fifth Amendment also says that the government cannot take away a person's "life, liberty, or property, without due process of law." This means that the government must follow fair and just procedures if it takes away a person's "life, liberty, or property." Finally, the Fifth Amendment says that if the government takes property from an individual for public use, it must pay that person an adequate sum of money for the property.

The Sixth Amendment requires that all criminal trials be speedy and public, and decided by a fair jury. The amendment also allows people on trial to know what offense they have been charged with. It also allows them to be present when others testify against them, to call witnesses to their defense, and to have the help of a lawyer.

The Seventh Amendment provides for a jury trial in all cases involving amounts over $20.

The Eighth Amendment forbids unreasonably high bail (money paid to free someone from jail before his or her trial), unreasonably large fines, and cruel and unusual punishments.

The Ninth Amendment says that the rights of the people are not limited only to those listed in the Bill of Rights.

Finally, the Tenth Amendment helps to establish federalism by giving to the states and the people any powers not given to the federal government by the Constitution.

After being approved by the House and the Senate, the amendments were sent to the states for adoption in October 1789. By December 1791, three-fourths of the states had approved the ten amendments we now know as the Bill of Rights. The Bill of Rights had become part of the U.S. Constitution.

How Our Court System Works

Many of the events in this book concern court cases involving the Bill of Rights. To help understand how the U.S. court system works, here is a brief description.

The U.S. federal court system has three levels. At the lowest level are the federal district courts. There are ninety-four district courts, each covering a different area of the United States and its territories. Most cases having to do with the Constitution begin in the district courts.

People who lose their cases in the district courts may then appeal to the next level in the court system, the federal courts of appeals. To appeal means to take your case to a higher court in an attempt to change the lower court's decision. Here, those who are making the appeal try to obtain a different judgment. There are thirteen federal courts of appeals in the United States.

People who lose in the federal courts of appeals may then take their case to the U.S. Supreme Court. It is the highest court in the land. The Supreme Court has the final say in a case. You cannot appeal a Supreme Court decision.

The size of the Supreme Court is set by Congress and has changed over the years. Since 1869 the Supreme Court has been made up of nine justices. One is the chief justice of the United States, and eight are associate justices. The justices are named by the president and confirmed by the Senate.

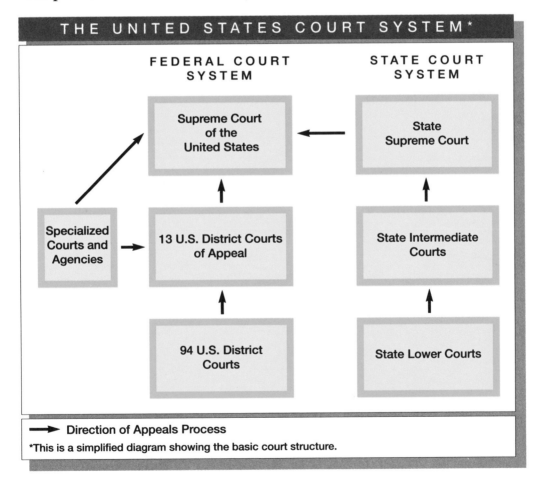

THE UNITED STATES COURT SYSTEM*

FEDERAL COURT SYSTEM

STATE COURT SYSTEM

Supreme Court of the United States ← State Supreme Court

Specialized Courts and Agencies → 13 U.S. District Courts of Appeal

State Intermediate Courts

94 U.S. District Courts

State Lower Courts

→ Direction of Appeals Process

*This is a simplified diagram showing the basic court structure.

In the Supreme Court, a simple majority of votes is needed to decide a case. If there is a tie, the lower court's decision remains in effect. When the chief justice votes on the majority side, he or she can assign the writing of the opinion to any of the majority justices, including himself or herself. The opinion states the Court's decision and the reasons for it. Who writes the opinion when the chief justice hasn't voted on the majority side? In that case, the longest-serving associate justice who voted for the majority decision can assign the writing to any of the majority justices, including himself or herself.

What if a justice has voted for the majority decision but doesn't agree with the reasons given in the majority opinion? He or she may write what is called a concurring opinion. That is one which agrees with the Court's decision but for different reasons.

Those justices who disagree with the Court's decision may write what is called a dissenting opinion. They have the opportunity to explain why they think the majority Supreme Court decision is wrong.

In addition to the federal court system, each state has its own system of courts. These systems vary from state to state. However, they are usually made up of two or three levels of lower courts and then the state's highest court, usually called the state supreme court. Those who lose their cases in the state supreme court may appeal those decisions to the federal court system, usually to the Supreme Court.

Not all cases that are appealed to the Supreme Court are heard by it. In fact, very few of them are. For the Supreme Court to decide to hear a case, four of the nine justices must vote to hear it. If fewer than four justices vote to hear the case, then the judgment of the lower court remains in effect.

The Second Amendment

Throughout much of American history, people have debated whether the right to own and use weapons should be given to everyone. The Framers of the U.S. Bill of Rights recognized this debate when they included "the right to keep and bear arms" in the Second Amendment. The right to own and carry those arms that could be used by a person serving in a militia is clearly protected by the Second Amendment. When it comes to other weapons and other rights having to do with weapons, disputes arise. Each side interprets the Second Amendment of the U.S. Constitution in ways that support its own position. For the past two centuries, Congress and the judicial system have worked to define the limits to the Second Amendment.

PHILIP A. KLINKNER

Historical Origins of the Second Amendment

"The great object is that every man be armed. . . . Everyone who is able may have a gun."

PATRICK HENRY

The Second Amendment to the U.S. Constitution has two main ideas: the need for a "well regulated Militia" and "the right of the people to keep and bear Arms [carry or be equipped with weapons]." The Second Amendment is the only amendment to the Constitution to include an opening clause that lays out the purpose of the amendment. The first part of the Second Amendment reads: "A well regulated Militia, being necessary to the security of a free State. . . ."

The word *militia* has several meanings. In its broadest meaning a militia is all the nation's able-bodied citizens declared by law as being subject to military service. By this definition, whether or not they are ever trained or called out to serve, everyone who is able-bodied is a member of the militia. A narrower definition of a militia is an organized group of citizens who have some limited military training. The group is called together periodically to practice defense skills. A government or state under threat can call out its militia for emergency service to protect the government's security.

Employments for Gentlemen in New England, a 1618 engraving by Theodore de Bry. In colonial times, those who could afford a firearm used it for hunting and for sport as well as for protection.

According to either definition, militia service is based on the idea that all men owe defense to their governments. Militias have almost always been for local defense and required only short terms of service. Members have regarded themselves as citizens first and soldiers second.

The second part of the Second Amendment states: "the right of the people to keep and bear Arms, shall not be infringed [violated or taken away]." The question of whether or not citizens have a right to be armed has been asked for as long as there have been governments to ask it. The answer depends on different things in different countries: the nation's history, economy, type of government, and social conditions.

The Framers of the Bill of Rights had specific reasons for joining the two ideas, the militia and the right to keep and bear arms. They had specific reasons for including the two joined ideas in the Bill of Rights. They were influenced by what was going on around them. They read history books and heard stories about the ways different governments had dealt with their armed citizens. A look at the history of ideas about arms and militia helps in understanding why these two particular ideas were included in the U.S. Bill of Rights.

Ancient Greece

Over 2,500 years ago, ancient Greece was made up of small independent cities, or city-states. In the Greek city-state of Athens, all the freeborn citizens came together to discuss important matters and make decisions. One decision reached by the citizens of Athens concerned the city-state's defense. It was decided that at the age of eighteen all able-bodied men would undertake two years of mandatory (required) military training. These servicemen made up the first organized militia of which we have written records. Of course, there were no guns in ancient Greece, but Athenian freeborn men were well armed with metal armor, shields, and long spears.

The number of freeborn citizens, or freemen, was very small compared to the large number of foreigners, women, and slaves in

Athens. It is estimated that in the fourth century B.C., slaves made up one-third of the Athenian population. One of the few times that slaves were granted the rights of citizenship was during wartime. Then they could take up arms alongside the freemen. In 338 B.C., at the Battle of Chaeronea, many (but not all) Athenian slaves were freed.

In the ancient Greek city-state of Sparta, there was a different arrangement. The city-state was defended by a group of full-time professional soldiers, a standing army. The strongest and fastest young Spartan men entered the army at age eighteen and served until age sixty. These young men did not choose to enter the army; it was chosen for them almost at birth. Boys were taught by their mothers to be brave and to handle the large battle shields, spears, and bows and arrows used by the Spartan army. As the defenders of Sparta, these soldiers and their wives made up the most noble and powerful class in the city-state.

Ancient Greek warriors used metal armor, shields, and long spears.

The examples of Athens and Sparta show two different ideas about armed defense. In Athens all citizens participated in decision making and defense, and all citizens were armed. In Sparta, on the other hand, only a select few were armed and involved in the defense of the city-state.

The Roman Empire

In Rome in the sixth and seventh centuries B.C., only those men born into certain powerful families enjoyed the rights of citizenship. Women were not citizens. The keeping of arms by individuals was recognized as a right of the Roman citizen. Carrying or using arms in self-defense was legal. But bearing a weapon with intent to kill was criminal. Every citizen had to give military service and be skilled in using the sword, axe, and bow for defense. The sixth Roman king, Servius Tullius, is said to have started a militia. Militia members provided and kept their own arms.

As Rome grew in size and power, a strict division of social classes developed. The Roman militia was replaced by a system more like that of Sparta. The oldest and most respected men became the Roman king's advisers and legislators. The younger able-bodied men became soldiers and knights—heavily armed men who rode war horses.

Before long, only those with a certain amount of wealth could serve as knights. The sons and relatives of the legislators and knights were known as patricians, or nobles. The farmers, the people who had been conquered by the Roman army of knights, and the people who came later to Rome were known as plebeians, or common people.

Only the wealthy upper class, the patricians, had the right to bear arms. The citizens' militia lost importance. A very large class of poor plebeians watched with envy as the rich patricians lived in luxury. The patricians had to rely more and more on a strong standing army to keep the unhappy and sometimes violent plebeians under control.

A Roman mosaic showing the Persians in battle against the forces of Alexander the Great in 333 B.C.

By the third century B.C., the plebeians had organized and successfully demanded some rights of Roman citizenship. The Roman government gave them almost equal voting rights with the patricians. Both plebeians and patricians could vote, but the weight of a vote depended on wealth.

With the Roman lower class satisfied, the Roman government could concentrate on foreign conquests. Rome's standing army conquered many neighboring states. Rome's territory grew larger and larger. Conquered states became Roman provinces, and the Roman Empire (group of provinces under the rule of a powerful leader or emperor) developed.

In about A.D. 100, when a great number of Roman citizens had been lost in foreign battles, Rome granted citizenship to some slaves and foreigners. These groups were then able to bear arms in the Roman army.

When the wars ended for a time, poverty increased in the Roman Empire. The empire became so weak that in the middle of the third century A.D., it was invaded by strong armies of barbarians (primitive foreigners) from the north. Many areas were violently attacked. Poverty, war, and disease killed many people. Travel became dangerous. Markets broke down, and trade between provinces was difficult. Slaves escaped from their masters. Cities emptied, and many schools disappeared. By A.D. 500 the Roman Empire had crumbled.

Feudalism in Europe

The Middle Ages in Europe, roughly from 450 to 1350, were full of bloody battles between rival armies, swift and ruthless raids by bands of armed horsemen, little organized government, and even less recorded history. There is little to suggest the existence of organized militias or restrictions on arms.

Gradually, what is now western Europe was settled into independent regions. Each region extended outward from a small walled city or castle. The form of government in the tenth, eleventh, and twelfth centuries was called *feudalism.* Feudalism was a political and military system in which free men traded their services for protection from violent invaders.

Feudal society was composed of lords, vassals, and peasants. A lord owned land, which he allowed a number of vassals to farm. In exchange the vassals were loyal to the lord. They promised to fight for the lord if his lands were attacked by invaders. Only noblemen or wealthy warriors were allowed to be vassals. Peasants could not become vassals. Instead, they worked for the vassals.

As feudalism developed, each vassal was required to provide an army of knights to defend the lord's land. This army was composed only of noblemen, who had the right to use battle weapons. The peasants gave up their right to use weapons and worked the land in exchange for protection by the noble army.

The vassal provided arms for his knights. Knights wore armor and helmets that completely covered their heads. They carried swords and crossbows, flexible wooden arms from which they shot arrows.

By the fifth century A.D., the area that would later become Great Britain came under the power of people called Anglo-Saxons, who had invaded from the north. As the Anglo-Saxons concentrated their power and settled down, they began a militia called the *fyrd*. The *wapenshaw* (a Middle English word meaning "weapon show") was a call twice a year for members of the fyrd to display their weapons. In that way military chiefs would know that their soldiers were adequately prepared for battle. There was no standing army or police.

Slowly the feudal regions in England were joined together under a single king. In 1181 under King Henry II a law was passed called the Assize of Arms. An *assize* was a session of a special court of

Süleyman the Magnificent's Turkish forces battle European Christians in the early 1500s. The weapons shown are swords, pikes, and spears.

justice. Certain statutes or laws that were written during such a court session were also called assizes. The Assize of Arms required that all free men have some type of arms. There were rules about the type of arms and armor that each subject (vassal of the king) could have in his home. The richer or more important the subject, the more weapons he could keep. All owners of weapons could be called upon for defense of the kingdom.

In another early law called the Statute of Northampton, which was passed under King Edward III in 1328, it became illegal to carry weapons, or bear arms, in public. "No man great or small . . . [shall] go nor ride armed by night nor by day . . . upon pain to forfeit [give up] their armour to the King and their bodies to prison at the King's pleasure." This law was designed to cut down on the number of robberies and murders. It appears that only honest people obeyed this early attempt at a weapons control law. Many people continued to bear arms in public. But the law clearly showed that the "right to keep and bear Arms" was not automatically granted.

It was during the 1300s, the last century that most feudal governments were in place, that the gun was invented. The early firearms were much more complex and difficult to make than the traditional swords and lances. They were also costly. The average poor farmer, peasant, or serf could not afford them. The feudal militias thus became weaker, because many of their members did not have guns. Governments could rely less on militias, so their armies became permanent forces. By the end of the seventeenth century, the "king's army" had become an established professional force.

Many people saw the deadly new weapons as cowardly and sinful when placed alongside the sword, the weapon of gentlemen. Until the eighteenth century the use of firearms, which were often seen as "unorthodox," or inappropriate, was limited by customs of war. Enemy soldiers captured with firearms were often put to death for using barbarous and ungentlemanly weapons.

The seventeenth-century militia in England in some cases combined the metal armor and pikes of medieval times with more modern firearms.

Rulers were practical about the use of firearms. If used properly by a ruler's army, firearms could be a great help. If firearms fell into the hands of people who disagreed with the ruler, however, they could endanger the government.

England

Many historians believe that the invention of firearms led to the development of modern European nations. The new weapons drove the knight from the battlefield. Those rulers who possessed firearms quickly gained great power. In England gun ownership was at first mostly limited to the wealthy and powerful. King Henry VIII tried to limit the new weapons, mostly because he was afraid that, if allowed to experiment with firearms, the common people would stop practicing with their powerful armor-piercing longbows. Then his militia, which still relied heavily on longbows, would become less effective. In 1541, however, when he found that he could not enforce the limits on gun ownership, the king allowed the ownership and use of most firearms.

A civil war that raged from 1642 to 1651 temporarily strengthened the English militia and spread knowledge of gun usage to common people. The same war led to the establishment of England's first standing army in 1645. Called the New Model Army, this military force supported the English legislative body—the Parliament—in a war against King Charles I.

The New Model Army was a great improvement on the Parliament's earlier armies. Its members were enlisted by the Parliament. It was more regularly fed and paid than any previous army had been. It was better disciplined. The New Model Army was able to defeat the king's army.

The leader of the New Model Army was Oliver Cromwell. He imposed martial law—the temporary rule by the military over the civilian population. The New Model Army was said to have treated the civilian population poorly. Many British citizens were angered. Trying to keep the country together, Oliver Cromwell dissolved the Parliament. He became a dictator.

The actions of Oliver Cromwell and the New Model Army made a lasting impression on the English people. The people were afraid of the power sometimes held by a leader with a standing army. That power could easily be misused. The English caution about standing armies crossed the ocean with those who were colonizing the New World.

In 1671 the English Parliament passed a Game Act that limited gun ownership. Guns, bows, and hunting dogs were forbidden to all those who did not own large amounts of land. Even rich city people were forbidden to hunt under the Game Act. The law linked the right to own and use firearms to the right to hunt, which only the wealthy landowners enjoyed. The law openly tried to keep those people who did not own land—whether they were poor or rich—disarmed. Not coincidentally, those who were allowed to use guns were the same groups that had gained political power in the sixteenth and seventeenth centuries.

King James II came to power in 1685 with the assurance that "I have often heretofore [until now] ventured my life in defense of this nation, and I shall go as far as any man in preserving it in all its just rights and liberties." As the English people soon discovered, however, their new king attacked their personal and civil rights and violated existing laws.

King James II hoped to make Roman Catholicism the most important religion in England. He prohibited all Protestants from owning arms. In a violation of the law, he only chose Roman Catholics to be army officers. He removed members of the Church of England from governmental and judicial positions. He put on trial Church of England bishops who disagreed with his decisions.

The king used the royal standing army, whose size he increased from 5,000 to 30,000 soldiers, to carry out his decisions. He was soon extremely unpopular and was distrusted by his subjects. Much of his army deserted him. James II was forced to leave England in what came to be known as the Glorious (and bloodless) Revolution of 1688.

A parliamentary committee of English citizens, remembering Cromwell and the New Model Army, as well as the more recent abuses by King James II, drew up a declaration that would become the direct ancestor of the U.S. Bill of Rights. The English Bill of Rights of 1689 condemned and tried to prevent abuses of power such as those by King James II. The English Bill of Rights proclaimed that "raising or keeping a Standing army within the Kingdome in time of Peace unlesse it be with Consent of Parlyament is against Law." This English Bill of Rights did contain a provision granting to Protestants the right to bear arms "for their Defence." But other English laws of the same period included specific provisions regulating firearms and hunting. There were also numerous acts prohibiting, or forbidding, people to go anywhere at night armed and an old common law prohibition against "going armed in terror of the people."

English common law is the law that came to be accepted through custom or court opinions rather than through legislation. Much of it was organized and written down in the seventeenth and eighteenth centuries by Sir William Blackstone. Blackstone included the right to bear arms in his lists of common law rights. He said that "having and using arms for self-preservation and defense" was among the "absolute rights of individuals."

Regulation of gun ownership existed in other parts of Great Britain. In British-ruled Ireland, the Parliament passed an act "for the Better Security of the Government, by Disarming the Papists" in 1695. The Protestant majority saw Roman Catholics, also known as "papists," as having different ideas and receiving the support of other Roman Catholic governments on the European continent. The 1695 act forced Roman Catholics to turn in all arms, armor, and ammunition. In 1739 a new law was added requiring yearly searches of Roman Catholic homes for arms.

Thus the British subjects who colonized the New World came with defined ideas about militias and gun ownership. They were used to laws and decrees concerning these. But the situation they found when they landed in North America was a far cry from the civilized England they had left.

Colonial America

The colonists who came to settle the New World arrived in what they considered a wilderness. It certainly was very different from the world they had left behind. Unlike Europe where hunting privileges were limited to the wealthy, in colonial America hunting was a necessary part of life. Most people hunted, and much of the land was open to public hunting. There are accounts of early colonial families who lived for nine months each year only on the meat from deer they shot.

The colonists also needed defense against the Native Americans who met them when they arrived in the New World. Millions of Native Americans had lived on this continent for thousands of years, hunting, gathering, and farming. When the colonists first arrived, most Native Americans had been kind and friendly. But in many places colonists tried to enslave them, take their land, burn their houses, and kill anyone who resisted. Often Native Americans responded by fighting against the settlement of white colonists on their land.

Native Americans, of course, knew much more about the local land, animals, and woods than did the colonists. Just as the colonists had become a threat to them, they became a real threat to the inexperienced European colonists. In some areas, both the Native American peoples and the colonists mounted fierce attacks on each other. At first, the Native Americans attacked with bows and arrows and spears. The colonists used muskets—six- or seven-foot-long firearms that were loaded from the muzzle end with round metal balls—that they had brought from Europe. By the age of twelve or thirteen, many colonial boys knew how to shoot a musket and were ready to join the fight. The only thing that kept the colonists from being massacred was their firearms.

Since guns came to be such an accepted part of early colonial life, settlers saw themselves as having the right to bear arms. In fact, some colonial governments actually required the bearing of arms. In 1623 Virginia forbade its citizens to travel unless they were "well armed." In 1658 it required each household to have a working firearm in the house, and in 1673 it began to pay for guns in households that could not afford them. In Massachusetts the legislature in 1644 decided to fine any citizen who was not armed.

However, not everyone was either required or allowed to bear arms. To protect against slave revolts, colonial Virginia forbade African Americans to carry arms without their masters' permission. Pennsylvania had a similar law by 1700. Virginia also banned (forbade) the sale of arms or ammunition to Native Americans. Massachusetts required that Native Americans have a license to carry a gun in parts of that colony.

Nor was the right to use arms granted in all areas. By 1678 Massachusetts banned the shooting of guns "so near or into any House, Barn, Garden, Orchards or High-Wayes in any town or towns of this Jurisdiction [area within the power of the government], whereby any person or persons shall be or may be killed, wounded or otherwise damaged." Pennsylvania banned the firing of a gun within the city of Philadelphia without a special license from the governor.

Colonial governments realized the need for settlers to protect themselves and their governments. Before 1763 a permanent garrison of British troops existed only in New York. So, in most cases, British troops could not be called to repel Native American attacks on the colonists. Over the years Native Americans were able to buy or trade for English and French guns. For protection the settlers in each of the colonies formed themselves into militias. Militias were the official military force in the colonies. The militias were made up of all white men between the ages of sixteen and sixty, who brought their own guns into service.

The separate colonial groups were disorganized and not always orderly. In 1757 William Pitt tried to reform the colonial militias. But they were still in poor shape when the American Revolution broke out in 1775.

When the fighting first broke out between American patriots and British troops, the colonial militias were the only American defense. At a minute's notice the "Minutemen" came out to fight when the British neared their homes. As the war progressed, the Patriots established a regular Continental Army, which drew heavily from the ranks of the colonial militias. Militiamen formed almost half of the Continental Army.

The experience of the American Revolution, where a "well regulated Militia" of all armed and able-bodied citizens proved very important, combined with knowledge of other militias in history to influence James Madison and other Framers of the Bill of Rights to include the Second Amendment in their document.

CHAPTER 2

The Birth of the Second Amendment

"What country can preserve its liberties if its rulers are not warned from time to time that its people preserve the spirit of resistance. Let them take arms."

THOMAS JEFFERSON

When they signed the Declaration of Independence in 1776, the colonial representatives were taking a great risk. The Declaration of Independence was a treasonable act against the government of Great Britain. The penalty for treason was execution and the giving up of all of the traitor's property to the British crown (the king or queen's government).

One of the complaints in the Declaration of Independence was about the British use of a standing army in peacetime. The Declaration of Independence demanded that the British government accept in America a principle accepted in Great Britain. Britain's King George III, in the words of the declaration, had "kept among us, in times of Peace, Standing Armies, without the Consent of our legislatures." The signers of the declaration made perfectly clear that they did not want the king's army on American soil.

The Boston Massacre

One time that the presence of a British standing army had aggravated the colonists was in Boston in 1770. Over a year earlier King

In 1787, Daniel Shays's rebels attacked the federal arsenal at Springfield, Massachusetts, and fought against the local militia. Shays's Rebellion revealed the government's weakness under the Articles of Confederation.

George III had sent thousands of British soldiers to Boston to protect British officials who were being threatened by colonists. The colonists were upset with the high taxes being collected by the officials.

The arrival of the British standing army only made the colonists angrier. The king had no right, claimed the colonists, to station army troops in their town when there was no war going on. Tension in Boston grew greater and greater.

On March 5, 1770, name-calling and stone throwing broke out. A large crowd gathered around the British troops. The soldiers were ordered to stay calm, but the insults kept getting worse. Angry colonists hurled stones, and everyone shouted and milled around. In the midst of the confusion, someone called out, "Fire!"

In response to the call, which could have come from a colonist or from a frustrated soldier, the British soldiers shot their muskets into the crowd. When the shooting stopped, five colonists had been killed. The shooting came to be known as the Boston Massacre, and news of it spread quickly through the colonies.

The news of the Boston Massacre led to a great number of public discussions about the king's standing army. The Boston Town Meeting (city government) spoke out: "The Raising or keeping [of] a standing army within the kingdom in time of peace, unless it be with the consent of Parliament, is against the law."

Although they still thought of themselves as the king's subjects, the colonists resented very much the presence of British soldiers when there was no war going on and when no one had asked the colonists' opinion in the matter. More than ever the colonists were convinced that standing armies in peacetime were dangerous to democracy. More than ever they believed in common defense through citizen militias.

The colonists readied their muskets and rifles for use in their local militias. The muskets they used had long barrels that were smooth inside. The musket ball shot straight out of the barrel when the gun was fired. The musket was not very accurate, but it was easy to load. The rifle, on the other hand, had a barrel with spiral

The Boston Massacre of March 5, 1770, as shown in an engraving by Paul Revere. This propaganda piece shows British troops firing their muskets at the colonists. Five colonists were killed.

grooves called *rifling* inside. The rifling inside the barrel gave a spinning motion to the bullet when fired. Rifles were much more likely to hit a target, but they were difficult for the colonists to load quickly.

The American Revolution started in April 1775, over a year before the Declaration of Independence was first read publicly. The colonial militias proved themselves in important battles. With help from France, Spain, and the Netherlands, the colonists won the war. When the Revolution ended in 1783, the Continental Congress, which had directed the war effort, continued as the central government of the newly independent nation. The members of Congress set about the difficult and complicated tasks of bringing the states together into one nation and creating a brand-new national government. And one of the issues they had to face, now that the British standing army had been defeated, was the new government's need for a permanent American standing army.

Shays's Rebellion

Despite their very strong feelings about the British standing army, Congress realized the need for a national force that could be called on immediately. It put its trust in militias, which were an important part of the young nation's history. Until the 1740s, when Great Britain began to send regular soldiers, the colonial militias had served as the only form of common defense. And again, when the Revolution ended in 1783, the Continental Army was allowed to shrink to under 100 soldiers.

During the Revolution, the new U.S. government was laid out by the Continental Congress in a plan called the Articles of Confederation. Congress approved the Articles in 1777, and the states ratified it by 1781. The Articles established a form of government like a "league of friendship," a loose grouping of largely independent states. The states were more powerful than the federal government. The federal government had no power to collect taxes or to set up a judicial system. Under the Articles of Confederation, the right of the states to maintain independent militias was clearly established.

Although the Congress wanted very much to rely on them, it soon realized that the state militias were not enough. One reason for this realization was Shays's Rebellion.

In September 1786 Daniel Shays and other local leaders in western Massachusetts led a group of several hundred armed men into the state capital of Springfield. The men were protesting because the local economy had become depressed after the war ended. They were unable to pay off their debts. The result was that the men's farms were being taken away. The armed group took over the state supreme court and forced it to close. That stopped the legal proceedings to take the men's farms.

In January 1787 Shays again was at the head of a protest group. This time he led 1,200 men in an attack on the federal arsenal in Springfield, Massachusetts, where many weapons and much ammunition were stored. He and his followers were pursued by the local militia, but he managed to escape to Vermont.

The national Congress was scared by Shays's Rebellion. Its members decided that the local militias and the leftover Continental Army, which had fought in the Revolution, were not enough. They wanted to rely entirely on armed citizens who formed themselves into militias. But many members of Congress realized that the nation's defense—against threats from the inside and out—required a more serious and organized army. In fact the weakness of the new nation and its army was one of the main reasons that the Congress called for a Constitutional Convention. It hoped that the Constitution would make the new nation stronger.

Army and Militia in the Constitution

At the Constitutional Convention controversy was strong around the issue of maintaining a standing army. As they discussed and wrote the Constitution, those Founding Fathers who favored a strong federal government—the Federalists—wanted to keep some type of standing army. The Anti-Federalists—those who were in favor of the state governments being stronger than the federal government—wanted to rely on strong state militias for the defense of the new nation. To the Anti-Federalists the militias were an important symbol of state power.

The final decision was based largely on cost. It would have been very expensive to keep up a federal standing army. The new nation was not wealthy. So both Federalists and Anti-Federalists at first agreed that efficient state militias—which were cheaper to maintain than a standing army—should be relied upon for local defense.

The writers of the Constitution hardly discussed the right of the people to bear arms. The ownership and use of guns was so much a part of the way of life of the citizens of the young nation that it was taken for granted by the Founding Fathers that Americans had the right to keep and bear arms.

Instead, the discussions centered on how these armed Americans would fit into the defense of the United States. The outcome of these discussions was a compromise found in the Constitution in Article I, Section 8. Part of the new federal government, namely the Congress, was granted the power to raise and support an army and to call up the militias. To the individual states was given responsibility for appointing militia officers and training their militia. The power to manage the state militias was split by the Constitution between federal and state governments, in order to provide checks and balances on their use. For the time being, both the Federalists and the Anti-Federalists were satisfied.

As They Ratify the Constitution, States Suggest Right to Arms

The new national Constitution could not take effect until at least nine states ratified, that is, approved, it in special elections called conventions. The state constitutional conventions discussed ratification of the Constitution. During these discussions many people spoke of the need to include within the document more guarantees of individual rights. Such rights included freedom of speech, freedom of the press, and many other rights.

Many members of state conventions said that the individual citizen's right to bear arms should be included in the Constitution. There were practical, everyday uses for guns in early America. There was still fighting between settlers and Native Americans. The new nation's frontier, which was just over the Appalachian Mountains, had to be defended. If a home was broken into or a life was threatened, there was no police force to call upon. In addition to self-defense, people still relied heavily on hunting to provide enough food for their families.

Many state conventions also stressed the importance of the state militias to provide a balance against a national army. Remembering the ways that British monarchs had disarmed the British people, the state governments did not completely trust the new federal government. They feared that Article I, Section 8, of the new Constitution would not be enough to protect their militias. They knew that an armed citizenry would protect the liberties enjoyed by the states and keep the young national government from becoming dictatorial.

As the states discussed whether or not to ratify the Constitution, both of these issues—the individual citizen's right to bear arms and the need for state militias—were raised, often together. Five of the state constitutional conventions suggested specific wording to protect the people's right to bear arms. Suggestions came from the conventions in New Hampshire, Virginia, New York, Rhode Island, and North Carolina. Several state conventions, including those of Virginia and New York, suggested guarantees of state power over local militias. Other state conventions, including those of Massachusetts, Pennsylvania, and Maryland, discussed the issues but made no formal proposal.

New Hampshire was the first state to ratify the Constitution. It suggested adding a clause that said, "Congress shall never disarm any citizen, unless such as are or have been in actual rebellion."

The New York convention proposed "That the People have a right to keep and bear Arms; that a well-regulated Militia including the body of the People capable of bearing Arms is the proper, natural, and safe-defense of a free State." This proposal clearly shows the two questions being argued: first, the citizen's right to bear arms, and second, the government's need for a militia.

In Massachusetts Samuel Adams suggested that the "Constitution be never construed [understood] to authorize [give power to] Congress to . . . prevent the people of the United States, who are peaceable citizens, from keeping their own arms." His suggestion was not adopted (even he voted against it in the end). Yet it showed that the right of individuals to keep arms was under discussion in the state conventions.

To ensure the passage of the Constitution, the Founding Fathers promised to listen to the suggestions of the state ratifying conventions. They promised that after ratification of the Constitution, a

Bill of Rights would be written and added to the original constitutional text. Given the amount of state discussion of the right to bear arms, this right would almost certainly be included in the Bill of Rights.

Writing of the Second Amendment

Sure enough, when James Madison first proposed seventeen amendments to the Constitution on June 8, 1789, among his proposals was an amendment dealing with the right to bear arms. He asked that "[t]he right of the people to keep and bear arms shall not be infringed; a well armed and well regulated militia being the best security of a free country: but no person religiously scrupulous of [holding religious principles against] bearing arms shall be compelled [forced] to render [do] military service in person."

Of course, Madison was not the first person to consider the right to bear arms and form militias. As he began to write what would become the U.S. Bill of Rights, he found several models to help him. He looked at the English Bill of Rights of 1689. He also looked at documents written by early Americans. Many of the colonies had written their own Declarations of Rights during the Revolution. In fact, many of the colonies had included in their state constitutions statements about militias and the individual's right to bear arms several years before the writing of the U.S. Constitution.

Five state constitutions—those of New Hampshire, Maryland, New York, Georgia, and South Carolina—mentioned militias but did not mention the right to bear arms. Three state constitutions—those of Virginia, North Carolina, and Massachusetts—granted a collective right to bear arms for the defense of the state. Two state constitutions—those of Vermont and Pennsylvania—recognized the individual right to bear arms. Four state constitutions—those of Rhode Island, Connecticut, Delaware, and New Jersey—mentioned neither militias nor the right to bear arms.

The Virginia Declaration of Rights had come first. It had been written by George Mason. It had been adopted by forty-five members of the colonial House of Burgesses on June 12, 1776. It stated: "That a well-regulated militia, composed of the body of the people, trained to arms, is the proper, natural, and safe defence of a free State; that standing armies, in time of peace, should be avoided, as dangerous to liberty." It did not mention an individual's right to bear arms.

The Pennsylvania Declaration of Rights of 1776 had been modeled on the Virginia example, but it added an important introduction: "That the people have a right to bear arms for the defence of themselves and the state; and as standing armies in the time of peace are dangerous to liberty, they ought not to be kept up." For the first time in a declaration of rights in what had been a British colony, the right of the people to bear arms was legally guaranteed.

Congressman Madison considered all of these previous statements as he drafted what would become the Second Amendment. His draft led to much debate and many speeches in the new national lawmaking bodies—the House of Representatives and the Senate.

Congressional Discussion of the Meaning of the Second Amendment

Once drafted, the Second Amendment was the subject of hours of congressional debate. In the House of Representatives, Representative Elbridge Gerry of Massachusetts, who would later become vice president of the United States under James Madison, asked: "What, Sir, is the use of a militia? It is to prevent the establishment of a standing army, the bane [source of harm or ruin] of liberty. . . . Whenever Governments mean to invade the rights and liberties of the people, they always attempt to destroy the militia, in order to raise an army upon their ruins."

During congressional discussions it was suggested that the amendment call the militia "the best security of a free State." But the congressional leaders chose to say instead that the militia was "necessary to the security of a free State." Many of them thought a small standing army was also necessary to the new nation's security against Native American attacks and foreign invasions. By not choosing the militia as the "best" option, the congressional leaders left open the possibility of using other security forces, such as an army.

Congressional leaders wanted their militias to be "well regulated," to be organized and orderly, and to have enough training and experience in the use of firearms. They remembered the different state militias and how they had performed during the Revolution. Some militias had been well organized and well equipped. Others had been sloppy and unprepared for battle.

In the clause "to keep and bear arms," the Framers of the Bill of Rights provided for two separate rights: the right to keep arms in their homes or places of business and the right to bear arms in public. It was suggested that the amendment should limit the right to keep and bear arms only to those times when an armed citizenry was needed "for the common defence." But there were other reasons for having and using guns, such as hunting and self-defense. Congressional leaders could not agree on which reasons for having and using guns should be included in the amendment. They chose not to list any of them.

After congressional discussion and approval the final version of the amendment read: "A well regulated Militia, being necessary to the security of a free State, the right of the people to keep and bear Arms, shall not be infringed." The House of Representatives changed the order of the two clauses in Madison's original manuscript. A fourth clause was dropped from Madison's manuscript: "but no person religiously scrupulous of bearing arms should be compelled to render military service in person."

That clause, the most controversial part of the amendment, grew out of the pacifism of the Quakers in Pennsylvania. Their religion forbade them to take up arms. It was Elbridge Gerry who protested against this clause. He said that it might allow those in power to declare certain groups "religiously scrupulous" and keep them from bearing arms. Other congressmen feared that people "of no religion" would use the clause as an excuse not to bear arms in the militia. The Senate dropped this clause from the Second Amendment during its ratification discussions.

In its final wording the Second Amendment clearly linked an established militia, which was important to the new nation's security, with the people's right to bear arms. The defense of the young United States depended on "a well regulated Militia." Guns were needed and used by most Americans. So for many years the wording of the Second Amendment would not be questioned.

The Militia Act of 1792

Soon after the Bill of Rights was ratified in 1791, Congress passed the Militia Act of 1792. It required that every free, able-bodied white male citizen between the ages of eighteen and forty-five be enrolled in the militia of his state. Each man was to provide his own weapons, as well as two flints and twenty-four rounds of ammunition for a musket or twenty rounds for a rifle.

The first test of the Militia Act of 1792 came two years after it became law. Protesting against high taxes on whiskey, farmers on the western frontier threatened to block tax payments. Farmers in the region were far from the markets for their crops. Transportation was slow and expensive. It was easier and cheaper to ship whiskey (made from the farmers' grain) than grain to the distant markets. The Whisky Rebellion, as it came to be called, led President George Washington to call out 13,000 militiamen from Pennsylvania and other nearby states. This quick action ended the Whisky Rebellion. It proved that the new federal government could successfully use state militia to enforce the law.

The Militia Act of 1792 gave final control over militias to the states. As a result, for 111 years (a second Militia Act was passed in 1862 and the third and most recent one in 1903—see Chapter 4) a national militia could not exist, and the federal government could not use state militias unless given permission by state authorities. Together, the Second Amendment and the Militia Act of 1792 made it clear that the new nation was dependent on its armed citizens.

CHAPTER 3

The Nineteenth Century: Who Could Bear Arms?

"Persons of color constitute no part of the militia of the State, and no one of them shall, without permission . . . , be allowed to keep a firearm, sword, or other military weapon, except that one of them, who is the owner of a farm, may keep a shot-gun or rifle, such as is ordinarily used in hunting, but not a . . . weapon appropriate for purposes of war."

South Carolina law

In the early 1800s Timothy Dwight, an American preacher, poet, and professor, wrote:

To trust arms in the hands of people at large has, in Europe, been believed . . . to be an experiment fraught [filled] only with danger. Here by a long trial it has been proved to be perfectly harmless. . . . If the government be equitable [fair]; if it be reasonable in its exactions [demands]; if proper attention was paid to the education of children in knowledge, and religion, few men will be disposed to use arms unless for their amusement, and for the defence of themselves and their country.

This statement by Dwight was typical of opinions of his day. American freedom, recently won, was proudly cherished and protected. And Americans believed that their guns were central to their freedom. There was a strong American belief throughout the

---

Daniel Boone Escorting Settlers Through the Cumberland Gap (detail) painted by George Caleb Bingham. Settlers used firearms for protection and for hunting and sport.

nineteenth century that the act of keeping and bearing arms was an unquestionable right of American citizens, at least of white Americans.

Mass Production Makes Guns Available to Almost Everyone

In 1800 the United States was a small and isolated nation. The Revolution had ended less than twenty years before, and the Constitution of the new American government was just a decade old. The United States heard news of the ongoing wars waged by the French general Napoleon Bonaparte in Europe. People worried that the conflict could spread across the ocean to American shores. The United States increased guns and arms production.

This increase in production was made possible in large part by Eli Whitney and other inventors. They applied to guns the invention of interchangeable parts in the late 1700s. Before this time a rifle was a unique collection of handmade parts. Each part would only fit other parts of that particular gun. With the new technology many guns could be made with parts of exactly the same size and fit. That meant, for example, that a replacement part could fit all the guns of the same kind, not just one particular handcrafted gun.

Gun manufacture increased. Gun makers worked hard to advertise and sell their products. There were many new advances in technology. After the Civil War U.S. military arms were the best in the world and were exported to many countries. This leadership in gun manufacture continued until the 1880s. By that time U.S. manufacturing machinery had been sold to many European countries as well as to China, Japan, Chile, Canada, and Australia. Foreign companies and governments could thus make guns of a quality equal to that of U.S.-made guns.

The success of the U.S. gun industry made it possible for a large part of the growing U.S. population to own and use firearms. Guns were affordable and available to almost all Americans in the nineteenth century. Hunting and target shooting remained the most popular national sports well into the century.

U.S. Vice President Aaron Burr kills Alexander Hamilton during a duel in 1804. Hamilton had been a leading Federalist.

Dueling became a fashionable practice among gun owners from the end of the American Revolution through the 1880s. Most states did not pass laws prohibiting dueling until the middle of the nineteenth century. Alexander Hamilton, who had influenced the shaping of the Constitution and Bill of Rights with his Federalist papers, was shot and killed in a duel with Vice President Aaron Burr on July 11, 1804. His death was mourned, for he was a great statesman. But it did not lead anyone to question the people's right to possess or use dueling pistols.

Guns were, and still are today, classified according to size. The guns of the early nineteenth century were hand-carried guns, called "small arms." They included pistols, muskets, rifles, and shotguns. Shotguns fired a cartridge or container filled with gunpowder and small pellets called shot. When fired, the pellets spread over a wide area. It was thus easier to hit a moving target with a shotgun than with the single bullet from a musket or rifle. For this reason the shotgun became popular with hunters.

Later in the nineteenth century, pistols and revolvers (small arms with short barrels) came to be known as "handguns." Also, portable automatic and semiautomatic weapons were developed, which could fire many bullets quickly.

Further Development of the State Militias

In part the gun survived as an important personal possession because Americans could not rely on protection by the government. The armed strength of the United States was still principally in the militias. This situation was uncomfortable to the federal government. That was because the state militias were often undependable and sometimes broke the very laws that the government wanted to enforce.

In Europe, a long war between France and Great Britain continued. The United States did not want to get involved. It insisted on maintaining neutral rights for its ships. The farming regions west and south of and including Pennsylvania favored war against Great Britain. Western settlers hoped to gain British-controlled lands, even Canada. They believed that the British were arming the Native Americans and encouraging them to attack American settlers. Native Americans also attacked across the border of Spanish-controlled East Florida. The New England states and New York were most affected by British attempts to interfere with American trade and shipping. These states opposed a war with Great Britain.

In 1812, President James Madison asked the Congress to declare war. Within weeks, Congress did. The War of 1812 was the first major war fought by the United States under its new Constitution. The main reason the United States gave for declaring war on Great Britain was to defend its shipping and trade rights. British ships had been stopping U.S. ships in the Atlantic and seizing sailors. Great Britain had continued to trade successfully with Native Americans, who had recognized the advantages of firearms for hunting and self-defense. Native Americans traded valuable beaver furs to the English, in exchange for muskets and gunpowder.

When the war began, the U.S. army had only 6,700 men. Most were poorly trained and equipped. The war caused a real stir about federal control of state militia. Throughout the war the New England states refused to send their militias in response to the president's calls. The Massachusetts Supreme Court ruled that neither the president nor Congress had the right to decide when the state militia should be called. The Connecticut legislature decided that the Constitution only authorized the use of state militia for defense, and not for the offensive act of going to war.

These actions by state governments showed that the state militias were an uncertain tool in national conflicts. The performance of the various state militias that went to battle in the War of 1812 was also uncertain. The Americans won a great victory at New Orleans in 1815 thanks to a militia led by Andrew Jackson. On the other hand, failure of militia troops caused an American defeat in the Battle of Bladensburg (1814). Largely because of their uncertain performance, the state militias were never again used to the same extent in a national war.

Guns Seen as Necessary on the Western Frontier

As the American frontier expanded westward, guns were as necessary to the frontier settlers as they had been to the early American colonists. Similar threats existed. Settlers going west needed to hunt for food. As they took over Native American lands or disrupted Native American hunting grounds, the settlers needed to protect themselves from attacks. Between 1865 and 1890, the settlers and U.S. cavalry fought different Native American peoples in almost every western state and territory. It was not until the

Battle of Wounded Knee in South Dakota in 1890 that the last of the Native American peoples were finally defeated. Then the settlers lost one of their key reasons for being armed.

In 1848 the United States defeated Mexico in a war that resulted in the gaining of vast new western lands. In 1849 gold was discovered in California. Thousands of people headed west to settle the land or search for gold.

In 1849 the U.S. Congress passed a law allowing people who were moving to the territories of Oregon, California, and New

In cow towns of the Old West, as well as in mining towns of the Far West, many people carried guns.

Mexico to receive surplus army weapons. The Congress felt that these people needed more guns for protection on their trip westward than they were able to afford. In this way the tradition of depending on armed citizens, rather than a standing army or police force, was continued.

In the Far West practically everyone carried and used a gun. A writer in San Francisco, California, in 1854 noted that "it has always been a practice with a large proportion of the citizens to carry loaded firearms or deadly weapons concealed about their person, this, being, as it were, a part of their ordinary dress."

Local western governments tried to restrict gun ownership and usage, but with little success. In Abilene, Texas, sharpshooters and cowhands shot to bits the posted notices that the carrying of firearms was prohibited. In many areas of the West the law was really much less important than who had the fastest draw and the best aim.

Gun Usage in the East

In the established eastern cities the use of guns was much more limited than in the Wild West. Rifles weren't often used. Native Americans in the eastern United States had long since been conquered. There was no longer a need to hunt for food. Some people armed themselves for self-protection with small pistols. These could be easily hidden from view. Of course, in both the cities and the countryside and throughout the nation, there were many criminal users of guns. In general, though, law-abiding city dwellers in the East stopped keeping and bearing arms in the early 1800s.

Cities grew quickly in the early part of the nineteenth century. Many people crowded into them, and violence followed. In Cincinnati in 1841, there were race riots in which both whites and blacks were heavily armed. One witness to an anti-Roman Catholic riot in Philadelphia in 1844 said, "These are strange things for Philadelphia. We have never had anything like it before, but now that firearms have been once used and become familiar to the minds of the mob, we may expect to see them employed on all occasions, and our riots in the future will assume a more dangerous character." Often state militias were called in to put down the riots and strikes.

Second Amendment for Whites Only

While white men and women living in the first half of the nineteenth century enjoyed the right to own and use guns, this same right was often denied to others. On the one hand, neither African Americans nor Native Americans were considered U.S. citizens by many people. On the other hand, the Second Amendment was not applied by the courts to state governments. Before 1868 (and actually even into the 1920s and 1930s), the Second Amendment was interpreted to apply only to the federal government. Any *state* could have disarmed *all* citizens, white, black, or other, without the slightest *federal* constitutional problem. In Louisiana, for example, in the early 1800s the so-called "slave codes" permitted free blacks to carry weapons only if they received a permit from a justice of the peace. Slaves were forbidden to carry arms.

On March 6, 1857, the U.S. Supreme Court, in its decision in the *Dred Scott* case, ruled that blacks, whether free or slave, were not entitled to the rights laid out in the U.S. Constitution, which includes the Bill of Rights. Chief Justice Roger B. Taney (pronounced TAW-nee) wrote that blacks had "no rights which any white man was bound to respect." The judicial branch of the national government was making a clear statement: African Americans were not to have constitutional rights, including the right to bear arms.

Even in the North, where there were many freed slaves and abolitionists (people who spoke out for an end to slavery), blacks were still often denied the right to bear arms. When the Civil War broke out in 1861, President Abraham Lincoln called for 75,000 militia soldiers to be assembled. Only white volunteers were accepted at first.

Large-scale recruitment of African Americans as soldiers in the Northern armies did not begin until after the 1863 Emancipation Proclamation. In 1864 Congress passed a law requiring equal pay for soldiers whether white or black. But the military units were racially segregated.

When there weren't enough Union soldiers, Congress passed a new Militia Act in July 1862. This new act stated that the militia would include all male citizens between the ages of eighteen and forty-five. No longer were black men excluded from militia service, at least in the North.

Because many state militias were no longer "well regulated," the new Militia Act also gave the president power to act to correct problems in any state militia. This power signaled a change in control of the militias. Until 1862 each state had controlled its own militia. From this time forward, however, the control would gradually shift to the federal government.

By 1863 Union authorities were organizing many black regiments. In all, 200,000 African Americans served in the Union armed forces, and 38,000 were killed. In the Confederacy a law allowing slaves to be enlisted as soldiers was signed in March 1865, but the war was over before this law had much effect.

Some believed that the Union won the war because of the arming of former slaves who had been emancipated, or freed. For example, that was the opinion of Senator Charles Sumner, a Republican from Massachusetts. It had been necessary, he said, "first, that the slaves should be declared free; and secondly, that muskets should be put into their hands for the common defense. . . . Without emancipation, followed by the arming of the slaves, rebel slavery would not have been overcome."

At the same time that blacks were being allowed to bear arms in defense of the nation, they were also taking up arms for self-protection. Even after the end of the Civil War, former slaves lived very dangerous lives. Over the next few decades several thousand African Americans were lynched—hanged, shot, or burned by angry mobs—mainly in the South. Frederick Douglass, the former slave who became a leading voice in the campaign to end slavery, publicly supported the right of African Americans to possess and use guns to resist kidnapping and slavery.

Part of the reason for the drive to give blacks the right to keep arms was for their own protection from the state militias and other armed white groups in the South. Before, during, and after the Civil War, Southern state militias often acted abusively against freed slaves. They would hang freed slaves or search their homes for arms. The Mississippi state militia took the guns of former black Union soldiers for its own use. According to a letter from a reader in Mississippi published in a weekly magazine in December 1865, "The militia of this country have seized every gun and pistol found in the hands of (so-called) freedmen of this section of the country. They claim that the Statute Laws of Mississippi do not recognize the Negro as having any right to carry arms.''

After the Civil War ended, Southern states began to pass laws restricting the freedom of former slaves. Similar to the slave codes enacted before the war, the laws were now called ''black codes.'' Among the laws were those that restricted weapons ownership by freed slaves. An act passed by Mississippi in 1865 said that ''no freedman, free negro or mulatto, not in the military service of the United States government, and not licensed so to do by the board of police of his or her county, shall keep or carry fire-arms of any kind, or any ammunition, dirk [a short, straight dagger] or bowie knife. . . .''

In South Carolina the law stated:

Persons of color constitute [make up] no part of the militia of the State, and no one of them shall, without permission in writing from the district judge or magistrate, be allowed to keep a firearm, sword, or other military weapon, except that one of them, who is the owner of a farm, may keep a shot-gun or rifle, such as is ordinarily used in hunting, but not a pistol, musket, or other firearm or weapon appropriate for purposes of war.

The U.S. Congress responded to laws such as the ones passed in Mississippi and South Carolina. First, it proposed the Thirteenth Amendment in early 1865. This amendment ended slavery in the United States. The states ratified it later in 1865.

Next, Congress passed the Civil Rights Act of 1866. The Civil Rights Act aimed to protect the rights of African Americans. It was the first law to declare that ''all persons born in the United States and not subject to any foreign power, excluding Indians not taxed'' were citizens of the United States. The act stated that all citizens ''of every race and color'' could enjoy the ''full and equal benefit of all laws and proceedings for the security of person and property, as is enjoyed by white citizens. . . .''

Another response to continuing restrictions on African Americans after the Civil War was the Fourteenth Amendment. This amendment was proposed in 1866 to add the principles of the recently passed Civil Rights Act to the Constitution, so that they could not be easily repealed (taken away). The amendment was supposed to guarantee the rights of U.S. citizenship. In 1868 the Fourteenth Amendment was ratified by the states.

For over sixty years, however, the Fourteenth Amendment was not to be interpreted as making the Bill of Rights apply to the states. In 1876 a case was brought before the U.S. Supreme Court that questioned the constitutionality of blacks being prevented from bearing arms for legal purposes. In its decision in *United States* v. *Cruikshank* (1876), the Supreme Court said that the Second Amendment only applied to the federal government (see Chapter 5). The states were for a time free to restrict arms ownership by their black citizens.

Native Americans and Gun Ownership

Even after African Americans gained the right to own arms, Native Americans were often still barred from gun ownership. The Indian Intercourse Act of 1834 provided the legal basis for Native Americans to buy rifles. But in 1835, according to U.S. Army documents, "the North Carolina legislature had designated the Indians along the Lumber River as 'free persons of color,' and had taken away their right to bear arms, as well as their right to vote. From time to time the substantial [wealthy] planters who sat on the Robeson County Court, would grant a permit to some Negro or Indian to own a firearm for such a legitimate purpose as shooting crows."

Also in 1835 President Andrew Jackson began a national policy of forcing Native Americans to move from the East to specific plots of land in the West called reservations. White settlers took over

Native American lands in the East. Guns were included in the list of provisions to be given Native Americans once they arrived at the reservations. The U.S. government was to provide "arms, ammunition, and other indispensable articles" to the Native Americans who moved. They were to be taught how to be gunsmiths. Steel and iron were to be purchased for them. By 1840 more than 60,000 Native Americans had been removed from eastern lands. Over half of that number had received rifles.

Many white settlers complained strongly about the arming of Native Americans, whose attacks they still feared. But other whites were glad to trade guns to the Native Americans. White traders could make large profits by trading guns for horses and mules, which the Native Americans stole by attacking U.S. and Mexican frontier settlements.

Mexicans living in the West also feared attacks by newly armed Native Americans. It was widely believed that by the 1830s several armed Native American peoples made a practice of stealing mules and horses from Mexicans in the region that is now Texas and New Mexico. The Native Americans traded the animals for guns and ammunition in Louisiana. As the frontier was pushed westward, trading posts were built as far west as Colorado, Oregon, and California. More and more white traders were providing guns and ammunition to Native American peoples. In some areas the weapons were used to hunt buffalo.

Some people, including the commissioner of Indian affairs, wanted a ban on the sale of arms to Native Americans. The commissioner in 1879 charged that "outside of Indian reservations, men are everywhere found driving a thrifty business in selling breechloading [in which ammunition is loaded from the rear, rather than from the barrel] arms and fixed ammunition" to Native Americans. The commissioner stated, "A law by Congress prohibiting under severe penalty the sale of both fire-arms and fixed ammunition to . . . Indians, is the only common-sense and practicable method of putting an end to this dangerous traffic."

Congress did not then legally limit the sale of arms to Native Americans. It did, however, pass a resolution in 1876 banning the sale of some types of ammunition to "hostile Indians" in Montana, Dakota, Wyoming, Nebraska, and Colorado. This ban on the sale of ammunition served to prevent the Native Americans from using the most modern guns of the time.

In 1884 the U.S. Supreme Court ruled that Native Americans, even if they left their tribes and lived among whites, were not U.S. citizens and therefore could not vote or bear arms. Not until the Indian Citizenship Act of 1924 did Congress grant U.S. citizenship to all Native Americans. And it was not until 1979 that special restrictions on Native American gun ownership were lifted.

Formation of the National Rifle Association

During the second half of the nineteenth century, the popularity of gun sports like hunting and target shooting led to the founding of organizations designed to promote shooting. The most important one was the National Rifle Association (NRA). The NRA was formed in 1871 by two U.S. military officers, Colonel William C. Church and George W. Wingate. In its early years, the NRA sponsored shooting matches and formed local rifle clubs.

When Congress in 1905 authorized the sale of surplus arms and ammunition to rifle clubs, the NRA was chosen to carry out the sales. By 1921 the NRA had about 3,500 members, most of whom were connected with the U.S. Army or National Guard. It was not until 1934 that the NRA became active in attempts to influence gun-related legislation. By this time the NRA had become the largest and best organized association of gun users in the United States. It first used its membership to influence Congress during debate over passage of the National Firearms Act of 1934.

During the nineteenth century, then, the Second Amendment's clause about the necessity of the militia became less and less important. More important was defining who would be included among "the people" who were allowed to enjoy "the right" to keep and bear arms. Although the phrase would not be widely used until the twentieth century, the U.S. government and the state governments practiced "gun control" by keeping African Americans and Native Americans from owning or using guns.

CHAPTER 4

The Second Amendment and Twentieth-Century Laws

"By calling attention to a well-regulated militia for the security of the Nation, and the right of each citizen to keep and bear arms, our Founding Fathers recognized the essentially civilian nature of our economy. . . . [T]he amendment still remains an important declaration of our basic military-civilian relationships. . . . For that reason I believe the second amendment will always be important."

JOHN F. KENNEDY

It was just about the beginning of the century that Americans first began to worry about firearms and their place in American life. There were several reasons for the new questioning of the people's right to bear arms. Law enforcement had become more professional and effective, and the frontier was settling down. Most people no longer depended on hunting for part of their food supply. The need for citizens to arm themselves for self-protection and defense was no longer so clear. On the other hand, a series of events took place, including several violent demonstrations during economic downturns, an increasing crime rate, and the assassination of President William McKinley in 1901. These events scared the American public into questioning the easy availability of dangerous weapons.

The Sullivan Law

As the public began to question the need for an absolute right to bear arms, its concern led to new laws. In the early 1900s states

---

These members of the National Guard are in cold-weather training in Alaska. In 1903 and 1933, Congress passed laws defining the role of state militias and the National Guard.

73

began to regulate or prohibit certain kinds of arms. In 1907 Texas placed a heavy tax on gun merchants. Oregon passed a law in 1913 requiring a person to get a license before he or she could purchase a handgun. New York passed the so-called Sullivan Law.

The Sullivan Law was named for New York State Senator Timothy D. Sullivan. The law passed the New York state legislature in May 1911 with very little opposition. Its passage was helped by media coverage of a string of shootings in New York City.

The Sullivan Law was the first law in the country to regulate not only the carrying of deadly weapons but also their sale and possession. The law made it a felony (a serious crime) for a person to carry a pistol or any concealed (hidden) weapon without first getting a special permit. City residents had to have a permit just to own a concealable firearm.

This was the most any state government had tried to limit the people's right to bear arms. Until its passage the provisions of the Sullivan Law were not well understood and not taken seriously. Once it became law and police began to arrest people with now illegal guns, there were serious protests about the Sullivan Law. It was called "vicious" and "an outrage against the rights of all American citizens." But the law remained on the books, surviving many tries at repealing it and several court challenges.

Federal Gun Laws in the Twentieth Century

By the end of World War I in 1918, 50,000 American soldiers had been killed in battle. Americans were depressed and bitter. Across the country, working people were becoming frustrated with poor working conditions. Factory workers joined unions and organized strikes. Hundreds of thousands of workers went on strike against their factories. Since working people, factory owners, and police all could carry guns, the strikes were often violent.

The number of crimes in the United States seemed to increase greatly. Even the established eastern cities experienced daily holdups, gun battles in the streets, and fast, cross-country pursuits.

Fear of the national crime wave and of violent strikes led to new laws limiting the right to bear arms. During the 1920s seventeen states passed major laws regulating gun ownership and use.

Even at the national level there was concern about unlimited gun ownership. The very first small step toward federal gun control laws was taken in 1919 with the passage of the War Revenue Act. This act was passed to raise money for a federal treasury strained by World War I. It placed a 10 percent tax on firearms sales.

During the twenties the U.S. Congress introduced a great number of laws regulating the sale and possession of guns. Thirteen were introduced in the House of Representatives in 1924 alone. Most of the proposed laws never got far. Only one proposal received serious attention. The Miller bill, introduced by Representative John F. Miller from the state of Washington, proposed strong limits on sales of guns through the U.S. mail. The bill was supposed to help states and towns that had passed gun control laws by reducing the flow of firearms mailed into these areas.

The Miller bill gave the U.S. Congress its first chance to discuss in detail the constitutionality of laws restricting the right to own and use firearms. Some lawmakers argued that the laws were unconstitutional. They said that such laws would seriously limit the personal liberties of U.S. citizens.

The strongest opponent of the Miller bill was Congressman Thomas Blanton of Texas. He said:

> I hope that every American boy, whether he is from Texas, New York, or Washington, will know how to use a six-shooter. . . . I hope every woman in America will learn how to use a revolver. I hope she will not use it but I hope she will know how. It will be for her safety; it will safeguard her rights and it will prevent her rights from being jeopardized. That is what the framers of this Constitution had in mind when they said the Congress should never infringe upon the right to keep firearms in the home.

Despite opposition the Miller bill was signed into law in 1927. With it Congress made it illegal for private individuals to receive concealable guns through the mail.

From 1920 to 1933 the Eighteenth Amendment was in effect. It prohibited the making, sale, and transport of alcoholic beverages. The period of Prohibition created a new criminal—the bootlegger—who provided people with illegal alcohol.

The Great Depression, which lasted from 1929 to 1941, was an economic slump in North America, Europe, and other industrial areas of the world. At its worst, one out of every four U.S. workers was unemployed. There was much fear that the hungry and the unemployed would become violent.

During Prohibition and the Great Depression criminals made earlier crime waves look unimportant. The weapons they used—sawed-off shotguns, silencers, and submachine guns—became known as "gangster weapons." These weapons appeared to be something that no law-abiding citizen could need. The American

A murdered gangster in New York City, 1936. Such "rubouts" of individuals by organized crime often made the headlines.

public began to demand restrictions on the sale and possession of weapons that were favored by criminals.

In response to this public demand, Congress passed the National Firearms Act in 1934. It was the first federal law to restrict the keeping and bearing of arms. By placing a $200 tax and a registration requirement on "gangster weapons," it was supposed to end private ownership of machine guns, sawed-off shotguns, silencers, and other weapons used by gangsters. It required the payment of a tax when certain firearms—any shotgun or rifle having a barrel of less than eighteen inches in length or any fully automatic weapon (including machine guns and submachine guns)—were transferred to another owner.

The 1934 law was followed by the Federal Firearms Act of 1938. This law gave the federal government a much larger role in controlling gun sales and ownership. Gun makers and dealers were required to obtain a license. They were not allowed to ship a gun across state borders to anyone charged with a crime or to convicted criminals.

With the National Firearms Act and the Federal Firearms Act, Congress made clear its belief that the Second Amendment did not prohibit it from restricting the sale and possession of firearms. There was not another piece of important gun-related legislation passed for thirty years, until the Gun Control Act of 1968.

The American Militia Changes Form

The U.S. war with Spain in 1898 sparked changes in U.S. law on militias. The Militia Acts of 1792 and 1862 were repealed. On January 21, 1903, Congress passed a new law that placed the state militias under the authority of the nation's president, creating a national reserve force. The new law provided that, unless the state chose another name, the militia of each state would be known as the state's National Guard.

The president drafted members of the state militias into federal service during World War I. In 1933 state militia units for the first time became official parts of the U.S. National Guard.

World War II broke out in 1939 in Europe. The United States became involved in the war when Japan attacked the U.S. base at Pearl Harbor in Hawaii in 1941. In response to the attack, the U.S. government called on its unorganized militia of individually armed citizens. There were not enough soldiers in Hawaii to fight against a Japanese invasion that was expected to follow the attack on the U.S. base. The governor of Hawaii therefore called upon individual citizens to use their own personal arms to run checkpoints and patrol remote beaches.

Today the National Guard system is considered by both the federal and state governments to be the natural descendant of traditional American militias. In fact, a recent U.S. Supreme Court decision—*Perpich* v. *Department of Defense* (1990)—held that members of state National Guard units continue to satisfy "the traditional understanding of the militia as a part-time, non-professional fighting force." In general state governments have come to call their organized militias by the name "National Guard." All of the weapons used by the U.S. National Guard are owned and controlled by the federal government.

The demand for war weapons during World War II allowed the American arms industry to grow quickly. Arms factories were expanded. Even when the war ended, the increased manufacturing of guns continued. Veterans of the war brought home military training and an interest in guns and other arms. Many brought back military weapons as souvenirs of the war. The U.S. government sold many more military weapons as surplus after the war. Gun ownership and use was respected and accepted by most Americans. Some changed their opinion after the assassination of President John F. Kennedy in 1963.

Assassinations Lead to Gun Control Laws

President Kennedy was shot while riding in a motorcade in Dallas, Texas, on November 22, 1963. He died almost immediately. Lee Harvey Oswald, arrested for the murder, was shot and killed two

President John F. Kennedy in Dallas shortly before he was assassinated in 1963. Within days after his death, gun control bills were discussed in Congress, but none of them was passed.

days later in the Dallas police station by a bystander, Jack Ruby. Ruby was convicted of murder and died in prison.

Public anger over the assassination, which had been committed with a mail-order Italian rifle, was very strong. The magazine of the National Rifle Association (NRA) reported that "never before has there been such a wave of anti-firearm feeling, or such a vocal and almost universal demand for tighter controls over the mail-order sales of guns." Within a week of President Kennedy's death, a dozen gun bills had been proposed in the U.S. Congress. Congressional debate over the new bills lasted four years.

Almost every person involved in the debate quoted the Second Amendment. Every person interpreted it to suit his or her position. Said Representative John Lindsay of New York:

Today the Nation no longer depends on the citizen's weapon, nor does the citizen himself. And, most significant, the population is now densely packed into urban areas, and it is diverse and mobile. In our changed and complicated society, guns have become more dangerous, and they demand more careful use. The Constitution must be interpreted in the light of the times; protection today means the reasonable regulation of firearms—not the absence of regulation.

On the other side of the argument, Congressman John J. Flynt, Jr., said:

One of the prized possessions of Americans has been the right to own and possess firearms and to use these firearms in defense of country, in defense of home, in self-defense, provided that use is done in a legal and legitimate manner. The attitude toward firearms has become a historical tradition in the United States. I think it is safe to say that it represents a priceless freedom won by those preceding us as Americans, which few if any other nations enjoy.

After Kennedy's death, arguments in Congress against gun control were strong enough to keep any of the proposed federal laws from passing. But throughout the 1960s frequent public opinion polls showed that three out of four Americans favored strict gun control laws. Between 1965 and 1968 gun control laws were passed in several states, including major ones in Connecticut, Illinois, New Jersey, and New York. Tough new laws were passed in Chicago, Philadelphia, and New York City. Then the assassinations began again.

Senator Robert F. Kennedy, who was running for president, was shot and killed with a pistol in a Los Angeles hotel the night of the 1968 California presidential primary election. Dr. Martin Luther King, Jr., the Nobel Peace Prize winner and civil rights leader, was shot with a rifle on April 4, 1968, on the balcony of his second-floor motel room in Memphis, Tennessee.

In response to these assassinations, Congress passed Title IV of the Omnibus Crime Control and Safe Streets Act in June 1968. This law was in turn included as part of the larger Gun Control Act signed into law on October 22, 1968. The Gun Control Act of 1968 replaced the Federal Firearms Act of 1938 and put wider restrictions on sales of guns between states. The act banned mail-order purchases and sales of rifles and shotguns to anyone under the age of eighteen. It also banned the sale of imported "Saturday night specials," a type of inexpensive and poorly made small handgun. Another key part of the act required gun dealers to keep records of all gun purchasers.

The act specifically stated that its purpose was to help control crime and violence. It further stated that it did not intend to restrict the rights of law-abiding citizens "with respect to the acquisition, possession, or use of firearms appropriate to the purpose of hunting, trapshooting, target shooting, personal protection, or any other lawful activity." The act was not meant to "discourage or eliminate the private ownership or use of firearms by law-abiding citizens for lawful purposes." The NRA nevertheless called it "the most sweeping Federal legislation ever imposed on U.S. firearms owners."

The Civil Rights Movement and the Right to Bear Arms

The 1950s and 1960s, presidential and political assassinations aside, were decades of violence. Courts had ruled that blacks must share the same protection as whites under the law and have equal opportunities to participate fully in national life. These rulings led to violent clashes between whites and blacks. Some civil rights workers were beaten and murdered, and their homes were searched by angry whites. There were race riots in many cities. Dr. Martin Luther King, Jr., a beloved leader of the civil rights movement, was assassinated. His death sparked more riots.

Malcolm X, the African-American religious leader, stated that the "Constitution clearly affirms the right of every American citizen to bear arms."

Some black leaders reminded their listeners of their right to keep and bear arms. Malcolm X was a Muslim minister and African-American leader of a movement to unite blacks throughout the world. He taught African Americans about pride and self-worth. He made many white Americans angry with his sharp criticisms of their society. In 1964 Malcolm X said:

The Constitution of the United States of America clearly affirms the right of every American citizen to bear arms. And as Americans, we will not give up a single right guaranteed under the Constitution. . . . We assert that in those areas where the government is either unable or unwilling to protect the lives and property of our people, that our people are within their rights to protect themselves by whatever means necessary.

Malcolm X was assassinated on February 21, 1965.

A radical political organization, the Black Panther Party, was founded in 1966. One of its chief goals was to protect the black community from police actions that many blacks thought were brutal. The party supported gun use for self-defense and in response to people who oppressed the poor. The program of the Black Panther Party said: "The Second Amendment to the Constitution of the United States gives a right to bear arms. We therefore believe that all black people should arm themselves for self-defense."

During the same period the United States was heavily involved in an unpopular war in Vietnam. In 1968 there were 525,000 U.S. soldiers fighting on the side of the South Vietnamese government, but they were unable to defeat North Vietnam. Many thousands of civilians were killed, and entire villages destroyed. There were strong antiwar feelings in the United States, and in 1969 U.S. troops began to withdraw.

By 1973 most of the U.S. soldiers had come home. Most of them were young men. They arrived home to find that many of their fellow U.S. citizens thought that the war had been a mistake. They were not considered heroes as earlier veterans had been. Their use of military weapons was widely condemned.

Still More Attempts at Assassination

The pattern of assassination attempts, followed by congressional activity, continued into the 1970s. Alabama Governor George C.

Wallace was campaigning for the Democratic presidential nomination on May 15, 1972, when he was shot in Laurel, Maryland. The pistol shooting left him paralyzed from the waist down. In 1972 a federal bill that would have prohibited the sales of new handguns that could not be used for sporting purposes passed in the U.S. Senate. But the bill did not pass in the House of Representatives.

While he was president of the United States, Gerald R. Ford escaped two assassination attempts in one month in 1975. During the 96th Congress, in 1976, over two hundred bills dealing with federal gun control were introduced.

On March 31, 1981, President Ronald Reagan was shot in the chest by a bullet from a cheap handgun called a Saturday night special. Three other people were also wounded in the shooting. The worst injury was to the president's press secretary, James S. Brady, who was shot in the head and suffered serious brain damage.

That shooting led a congressional committee to draft a handgun crime control bill in 1981. The bill banned the sale of inexpensive, poorly made guns called Saturday night specials. It required a twenty-one-day wait before the purchase of any legal handgun. It banned gun sales by pawnshops. It also required a person convicted of using or carrying a handgun while committing a serious crime to serve a minimum jail sentence, in most cases five years. Largely because of strong arguments and lobbying by the NRA, the 1981 handgun crime control bill was not even voted on by Congress.

A Ban on Guns

In 1981 the town of Morton Grove, Illinois, a suburb sixteen miles from downtown Chicago, banned the possession of handguns by civilians. By doing this it became the first American government at any level to try to completely ban, not just restrict, a common form of arms since the Civil War. The law permits only licensed gun collectors, police officers, members of the armed forces and militia on active duty, and other specified people to keep handguns at home. It allows all other people to keep or use handguns at licensed gun clubs in the town.

Morton Grove was a quiet residential suburb. Guns were not unknown there, but they were not a big problem. By passing the handgun ban, the town's leaders were trying to keep Morton Grove, and especially its youth, from getting to know handguns.

A resident of the town had applied for a permit to open a gun store, close to the local junior high school. "We didn't want the kids looking in the window, dreaming of guns," said one town leader. "We wanted to stop that store." There was no local, state, or federal law that the town leaders could use to deny the permit. The only way they could stop the gun store was to ban the sale and private possession of handguns. On June 8, 1981, they did just that.

The law passed in Morton Grove, Illinois, led to similar laws in Oak Park and Wilmette, Illinois, and in other parts of the United States. A similar law was also passed in San Francisco, California, in 1982, but it was later overturned by a state court. Courts in Illinois, however, ruled that the Morton Grove law did not violate the Illinois Constitution, which has a clause similar to the Second Amendment of the U.S. Constitution.

Gun Awareness Programs

Unfortunately, in the United States by 1990 about ten children a day were being killed by guns. Over a hundred children a day were being seriously injured by guns. Some communities, choosing not to ban handguns, took other steps to prevent gun-related injury.

For example, the public schools in Dade County, Florida—the country's fourth largest school system—began a gun awareness program for all its students from kindergarten through twelfth grade. Through lectures, films, and skits children are taught not to play with or carry handguns. They learn about the dangers of guns and about gun safety. Their parents are provided with suggestions on how to prevent accidents with handguns in the home. Around the nation other school districts and police departments are considering adopting similar gun awareness programs.

The Second Amendment and the Courts

"In the absence of any evidence . . . that possession or use of a 'shotgun having a barrel of less than eighteen inches in length' . . . has some reasonable relationship to the preservation or efficiency of a well regulated militia, we cannot say that the Second Amendment guarantees the right to keep and bear such an instrument."

Opinion of the Court, *United States* v. *Miller* (1939)

The Second Amendment has been interpreted in many ways by students and teachers of law, lawyers, judges, ordinary citizens, and politicians. Between these groups there is often little agreement about what the amendment meant to the Framers of the Bill of Rights and what it means today. Thus one group may have a very different idea from another about the "right to keep and bear arms."

Despite or perhaps because of this wide variety of ideas about the Second Amendment, the U.S. Supreme Court has only rarely ruled on cases about the amendment. The Supreme Court often chooses instead to decline to make a decision. Since the Bill of Rights was ratified in 1791, the U.S. Supreme Court has ruled only five times on cases dealing with the Second Amendment. Only once has it made a decision that clearly defined what the Second Amendment could do.

Chief Justice Morrison R. Waite served on the Supreme Court from 1874 to 1888. The Court ruled in *United States* v. *Cruikshank* (1876) that "the right to bear arms for a lawful purpose" is not an absolute right. According to the decision, the Fourteenth Amendment did not prevent state governments from limiting their citizens' right to bear arms.

Unlike the U.S. Congress, courts of law generally do not base their decisions on public opinion or on current political activity. They instead rely on the facts of the particular case before them, including current laws, and on earlier court decisions called precedents. This is why the Supreme Court may appear to move at a different pace than Congress or the American public on the issues raised by the Second Amendment.

The First U.S. Supreme Court Case

Between 1876 and 1894, the U.S. Supreme Court dealt three times with cases involving the Second Amendment. The first case, called *United States* v. *Cruikshank,* reached the Supreme Court in 1876 on appeal from a Louisiana circuit court.

The case stemmed from an incident when a group of several hundred armed whites, led by a man named William J. Cruikshank, attacked a courthouse. Hundreds of blacks were holding a public assembly inside. The attackers burned down the courthouse and murdered about one hundred people. The group was accused of, among other things, attacking two black men, Levi Nelson and Alexander Tillman, and taking away their weapons. At the time Louisiana law limited weapon possession by blacks.

When it became a part of the U.S. Constitution in 1868, the Fourteenth Amendment was supposed to keep the state governments from threatening the individual liberties guaranteed by the Constitution. The Fourteenth Amendment said, "No State shall make or enforce any law which shall abridge the privileges or immunities of citizens of the United States. . . ." When the *Cruikshank* case reached the Supreme Court in 1876, the Court was asked to decide whether the Fourteenth Amendment prevented the Louisiana state government from threatening Second Amendment liberties by limiting gun ownership.

The Court did not look closely at the meaning of the Second Amendment. Its decision did not deal directly with the right to bear arms or the militia. It decided that the Fourteenth Amendment did not prevent state governments from limiting the Second Amendment rights of its citizens. The Court's 1876 decision stated that the "right to bear arms for a lawful purpose" is not an absolute right granted by the Constitution. Nor "is it in any manner dependent on that instrument for its existence."

The Court's opinion went on to say that the Second Amendment "means no more than that it [the right to bear arms] shall not be infringed by Congress. This is one of the amendments that has no other effect than to restrict the powers of the national government." The decision did not deal with how much the federal government is restricted by the Second Amendment.

The Court's decision meant that only the national Congress was bound by the Second Amendment. The rights of individuals were all "left under the protection of the States." The state governments would continue to be free to make their own laws about the possession and use of firearms. Thus individuals should look to their state law, not federal law, for protection of the right to bear arms.

The Case of *Presser* v. *Illinois*

The next case involving the Second Amendment was heard by the U.S. Supreme Court in November 1885. The case of *Presser* v. *Illinois* involved the charge that Herman Presser, a thirty-one-year-old man from Illinois, had organized and led through the streets of Chicago a company of about 400 armed men. The men, all German Americans, had formed their own mini-army. They carried rifles. But they were not part of the state militia or U.S. troops. They had no license from the governor of Illinois to drill or parade as part of the state's militia. Illinois law prohibited the creating or parading of a military group without such a license.

Presser claimed that the Illinois law was unconstitutional because it violated his Second Amendment right to bear arms. The U.S. Supreme Court disagreed and upheld the Illinois law. The Court's 1886 decision said that "the amendment is a limitation only upon the power of Congress and the National government, and not upon that of the States.''

The decision went on to say that

> it is undoubtedly true that all citizens capable of bearing arms constitute [make up] the reserved military force or reserve militia of the United States as well as of the States, and . . . the States cannot . . . prohibit the people from keeping and bearing arms, so as to deprive the United States of their rightful resource for maintaining the public security, and disable the people from performing their duty to the general government.

Thus state governments could not control the bearing of arms in such a way that the militia was no longer effective. But they could make it against the law for people to drill and parade with arms in a military group without permission. The Court said that the question of whether a state government may prohibit the citizens of that state from bearing arms for other than military reasons did not need to be addressed at that time.

The Court followed the interpretation of the Fourteenth Amendment laid out in *United States* v. *Cruikshank* (1876): ''A State may pass laws to regulate the privileges and immunities of its own citizens, provided that in so doing it does not abridge their privileges and immunities as citizens of the United States.'' In other words, the Fourteenth Amendment did not protect the right to bear arms as part of U.S. citizenship.

The Case of *Miller* v. *Texas*

In 1894 the U.S. Supreme Court heard the case of *Miller* v. *Texas*. Franklin P. Miller had been tried and convicted of murder and sentenced to death. On appeal he claimed that his Second Amendment rights had been restricted by a Texas law that prohibited people from carrying weapons in public.

The Supreme Court again stated that the Fourteenth Amendment does not apply the Second Amendment to the states. In this case the Court upheld the Texas law prohibiting people from carrying deadly weapons. The reason the Court gave was that the Second Amendment limits "operate only upon the Federal power, and have no reference whatever to proceedings in State courts."

The Case of *United States* v. *Miller*

In 1934 the U.S. Congress passed the National Firearms Act. It was the first federal law to restrict the keeping and bearing of arms. The constitutionality of this law was soon questioned. It was brought before the U.S. Supreme Court in the 1939 case of *United States* v. *Miller.* Jack Miller and Frank Layton were charged with transporting a sawed-off double-barrel shotgun across state lines without the registration and tax stamp required by the act. A district court had held that the law violated the Second Amendment and had freed Miller and Layton.

This case was the only time that the Supreme Court has ever ruled directly on the meaning of the Second Amendment. It was the only time that the Court faced a direct challenge to a federal law that might have limited Second Amendment rights. The Court overruled the district court. It decided that the National Firearms Act of 1934 was constitutional and did not violate the Second Amendment.

The Court reached its decision in two steps. First, it found that

in the absence of any evidence tending to show that possession or use of a "shotgun having a barrel of less than eighteen inches in length" at this time has some reasonable relationship to the preservation or efficiency of a well regulated militia, we cannot say that the Second Amendment guarantees the right to keep and bear such an instrument.

In other words the Second Amendment did not protect the right to own and use weapons—such as sawed-off shotguns—that were not useful to a militia.

Second, the Court explained why it had been necessary to show that the shotgun was not useful for militia service. It looked carefully at the first clause of the Second Amendment, "A well regulated Militia being necessary to the security of a free State." In its decision in *United States* v. *Miller* (1939), the Court talked at length about the history of militia in the United States and the fact that members of the militia were expected to provide their own arms.

The Court decided that the Second Amendment had been meant to address militia forces, "with obvious purpose to assure the continuation and render [make] possible the effectiveness of such forces. It must be interpreted [understood] and applied with that end in view." The Second Amendment was ruled to be a guarantee only of the right of state governments to maintain organized militia units free from federal control. The Court held that the right to bear arms is a collective or community right related to service in the militia.

Thus the Court ruled that the definition of firearms written into the National Firearms Act did not violate the Second Amendment. Congress could constitutionally regulate guns, and a gun tax could be used to control possession of certain kinds of firearms. The case of *United States* v. *Miller* (1939) did not deal with the issue of whether an individual has a guaranteed right to bear arms under the Second Amendment.

The Case of *Lewis* v. *United States*

The U.S. Supreme Court again touched on the Second Amendment in the case of *Lewis* v. *United States* (1980). Its decision did little to clarify previous decisions. George Calvin Lewis, Jr., had already been convicted of a major crime. This made him a convicted felon (person found guilty of committing a serious crime). He was arrested again in Virginia in 1977 and charged with having knowingly received and possessed an illegal firearm.

Title VII of the Omnibus Crime Control and Safe Streets Act, passed in 1968, prevented certain groups of people from having or using any firearm. Included in the group were convicted felons, soldiers who had been dishonorably discharged from the armed forces, mental incompetents, anyone who had renounced his or her U.S. citizenship, and illegal aliens.

The Supreme Court said that Title VII of the act had been enacted in response to a rise during the 1960s in assassinations, riots, and other violent crimes involving firearms. The Court pointed to the case of *United States* v. *Miller* (1939). It held that legislative restrictions on the sale and possession of firearms do not challenge the Constitution. Lewis's conviction was upheld.

Decisions of State Courts

Most of the court cases dealing with the meaning of the Second Amendment have been at the state and district court level. Forty-three state constitutions currently protect the right to bear arms in one form or another. They provide independent legal basis for many of the rulings discussed. While they have not directly challenged the Second Amendment itself, lower court cases have dealt with state and local laws limiting the right to keep and bear arms.

It was early in the nineteenth century that a part of the Second Amendment was first questioned in a state court. Still the individual citizen's right to keep and bear arms was understood to be constitutional. The question then being asked was how a person's weapons could lawfully be carried and used.

At first, state courts seemed reluctant to place limits on the Second Amendment. In 1813 Kentucky passed the first law in the United States forbidding people from carrying concealed weapons. In 1822 a Kentucky court made the first state court decision on the right to bear arms. In *Bliss* v. *Commonwealth* the court heard the appeal of a man who had been convicted of having a sword concealed as a cane. The Kentucky court freed the man when it decided that the right to bear arms could not be limited only to openly carried arms.

This case was decided on the basis of Kentucky's state constitution. The court decided that "the right of citizens to bear arms in defense of themselves and the State must be preserved entire. . . ." A Tennessee court agreed in 1833, saying that no limits were to be placed on the kind or nature of arms that might be owned or used.

In 1837 Georgia passed a law totally banning the sale of most pistols. In *Nunn* v. *State* (1846) the Georgia Supreme Court found the law unconstitutional under the Second Amendment. It said that the second clause of the Second Amendment meant that "the right of the whole people, old and young, men, women and boys, and not militia only, to keep and bear arms of every description, and not such merely as are used by the militia, shall not be infringed, curtailed, or broken in upon, in the smallest degree."

The Georgia court use of the U.S. Constitution's Second Amendment was not the usual practice of that time, the court admitted. It was, in fact, the only court case to try to apply the Second Amendment before the Fourteenth Amendment was ratified in 1868.

These early decisions were unique because they stated that the individual citizen's right to bear arms is absolute and unquestionable. Most later decisions at the state and local level have limited or reversed these decisions.

In the 1840s state courts began to restrict weapons usage. In *Aymette* v. *State* in 1840, the Supreme Court of Tennessee held that the right to bear arms was a collective right of the people to protect themselves from a repressive government. Its decision stated that "the citizens have the unqualified right to keep the weapon . . . but the right to bear arms is not of the unqualified nature." This was based on part of that state's own bill of rights. Some later court decisions have followed this idea. According to these decisions, arms can legally be kept, but their use can be regulated by the states to ensure the public peace and welfare.

An Arkansas court in 1842 upheld a state law that forbade people from carrying concealed weapons—but only if the weapons concealed were not suitable for use in a militia. In other words Arkansans were free to carry concealed weapons if the weapons were of a type that could be used in militia duty. In this way the linkage between the first and second clauses of the Second Amendment was respected. As time went on, every court except that of Kentucky (In *Bliss* v. *Commonwealth,* 1822) that has ruled on a concealed weapons law has found it constitutional.

Most of the state cases heard later in the nineteenth century took the position of *Commonwealth* v. *Murphy.* That case was heard by a Massachusetts court in 1896. The court said that "it has been almost universally held that the legislature may regulate and limit the mode of carrying arms." Courts ruled in 1872 that a state could prohibit people from carrying certain deadly weapons, ruled in 1882 that a state could forbid people from carrying concealed weapons, and ruled in 1911 that a state could require people to get a license before they could carry revolvers. A California court agreed in 1924 that the right to keep and bear arms could be restricted by the government: "It is clear that, in the exercise of the police power of the state, that is, for public safety or the public welfare generally, such right may be either regulated or, in proper cases, entirely destroyed."

Federal and State Court Cases in the Twentieth Century

In almost all lower court cases heard in this century, courts have continued to rule that the right to keep and bear arms can be restricted, or in some cases even prohibited, by the government. Some courts have ruled that individual citizens have the right to bear firearms for self-defense, but this right can be limited.

In 1942 the case of *Cases* v. *United States* was heard by a U.S. Court of Appeals in Puerto Rico. All kinds of weapons had been used by "commando units" in World War I, the case argued. Thus the limits placed by the decision in *United States* v. *Miller* (1939) on weapons having "some reasonable relationship to the preservation or efficiency of a well regulated militia" were outdated and had little or no meaning. Any firearm could be seen to have militia use.

The decision of the appeals court in the *Cases* case was that the Second Amendment did not give private citizens a right to possess deadly weapons of any kind. It did not matter whether or not they were the kind that would be useful to a well-regulated militia. "The right to keep and bear arms is not a right conferred on the people by the federal constitution," the court ruled. Following the logic of the *Miller* case, it decided that the federal government can *limit* the keeping and bearing of arms by an individual as well as by a group. But the federal government cannot *prohibit* the sale or possession of any weapon that could be used in a militia.

The case of *United States* v. *Warin* was decided by a U.S. Court of Appeals in 1976. Francis J. Warin had been convicted by a district court in Ohio of possessing a submachine gun that was not registered to him. Warin had appealed, arguing that he had made the gun himself. According to Warin, as an adult male eligible for service in the state militia he should be allowed to have such a weapon, which was standard for military use. He claimed that his conviction was a violation of his Second Amendment right to keep and bear arms.

The U.S. Court of Appeals upheld Warin's conviction. It said that "it is clear that the Second Amendment guarantees a collective rather than an individual right." It went on to repeat an earlier decision that "since the Second Amendment right 'to keep and bear Arms' applies only to the right of the State to maintain a militia and not to the individual's right to bear arms, there can be no serious claim to any express constitutional right of an individual to possess a firearm."

The U.S. Court of Appeals went even further. "Even when the Second Amendment is applicable, it does not constitute [set up] an absolute barrier to the congressional regulation of firearms," it ruled. The court realized that weapons such as the submachine gun

Federal and local officials view a huge arms cache seized from people attempting to sell the weapons illegally.

can pose a threat to society. There "can be no question that an organized society which fails to regulate the importation, manufacture and transfer of the highly sophisticated lethal weapons in existence today does so at its peril."

In a number of twentieth-century cases, lower courts have decided that the right to keep and bear arms protects the individual citizen's right to keep weapons—such as pistols and revolvers—for self-defense. The supreme courts of Colorado, Oregon, and Montana all made this decision when looking at their state constitutions, which have clauses similar to the Second Amendment.

In stating its decision in a 1980 case, the Oregon Supreme Court said:

We are not unmindful that there is current controversy over the wisdom of the right to bear arms, and that the original motivations [reasons] for such a provision might not seem compelling [forceful or strong] if debated as a new issue. Our task, however . . . is to respect the principles given the status of constitutional guarantees and limitations by the drafters; it is not to abandon these principles when this fits the needs of the moment.

The court obviously realized that its decision would be criticized by supporters of gun control. But it decided to stick to what it saw as the principles of the Framers of the Bill of Rights. It supported the right of the individual citizen to openly carry a gun for self-defense. But the right to carry concealed weapons has been routinely outlawed by state legislatures.

Court Appeals of the Morton Grove Handgun Ban

The Chicago suburb of Morton Grove voted in 1981 to ban the sale and possession of handguns within its limits. Opponents of gun restrictions then worked to have the ban declared unconstitutional. They argued that the Morton Grove gun ban was unconstitutional because it partially disarmed the unorganized militia of the United States. According to this argument, citizens of Morton Grove were therefore unable to perform their duty as members of the U.S. militia. Opponents also argued that Morton Grove could not pass laws that take away permanent rights guaranteed by the U.S. Constitution.

A federal district court in 1981 disagreed. It ruled in favor of the ban. A federal court of appeals heard the case in 1982. It also decided in favor of the ban. In its decision in the case of *Quilici* v. *Village of Morton Grove* (1982), it said of the language used in the Second Amendment: "Construing [understanding and explaining] this language according to its clear meaning, it seems clear that the right to bear arms is inextricably [in a way that cannot be separated] connected to the preservation of a militia." The court went on to rule that "the right to keep and bear handguns is not guaranteed by the second amendment."

This handgun is a .44-caliber revolver. Some local governments have passed laws limiting the right to keep and bear handguns.

In 1983 the U.S. Supreme Court refused to hear an appeal on the *Morton Grove* case (1982). The Court has in general been very reluctant to rule on cases involving further definition of Second Amendment rights. It appears that the Court will not rush to apply the Second Amendment to the states. As currently interpreted by the Supreme Court, the Second Amendment does not restrict Congress or state or local governments from limiting the right to keep and bear handguns.

CHAPTER 6

The Gun Control Debate

"The right to own and use firearms is the preeminent individual right. Without the ability to physically defend . . . our Constitution . . . , the remainder of the Bill of Rights become privileges granted by the government and subject to restrictions at the whim of the government."

J. WARREN CASSIDY, Executive Vice President,
National Rifle Association

"When the Constitution was drafted, our Founding Fathers foresaw a great nation of peace and tranquility. Part of the legacy of that vision is a nation free from violence. . . . The Courts agree that nothing in the Constitution prohibits legislators from enacting common-sense restrictions on firearms."

SARAH BRADY, Chairperson, Handgun Control, Inc.

Violent crime has been increasing in the United States. A number of important political and social leaders have been assassinated or shot at. The American public, scared by the trends in crime, has demanded that something be done. Some people have called for stricter, longer sentences for those convicted of violent crimes. Some have called for gun control

Gun control can mean many things. It can mean completely banning the sale or possession of all firearms, from pistols to shotguns to automatic assault rifles. It can mean limiting sales of guns to certain groups of people or requiring registration of guns by

---

Millions of dollars worth of firearms such as these assault weapons used by drug smugglers are seized every year by law-enforcement officials.

their owners. In short, gun control is any government action that limits in some way the possession or use of firearms.

The idea of gun control is not new. King Edward III of England controlled weapons with the Statute of Northampton in 1328. French monarchs in the sixteenth century ordered peasants and city dwellers alike to give up their guns. State governments in this country began to control firearms as early as 1813, when Kentucky banned the carrying of concealed weapons.

Because of public concern about laws dealing with crime, discussion of the Second Amendment since the 1960s has turned into a debate over gun control. People have looked to the Second Amendment to help them decide if gun control is constitutional. They have found very different answers.

Just as there are two parts of the Second Amendment, so are there two sides of the gun control debate. At the heart of the debate over gun control is interpretation of the Second Amendment's clause: "A well regulated Militia, being necessary to the security of a free State. . . ." Those who oppose gun control see the opening phrase of the amendment as a simple statement of purpose. Taking the "individual right" view, they argue that the Second Amendment absolutely protects the right of individual citizens to own and use guns without restriction by the government. Any such restriction, they say, would reduce an individual liberty guaranteed by the Constitution.

Those who favor gun control place much emphasis on the first clause of the Second Amendment. They take the "collective right" view that, because of its introductory clause, the Second Amendment protects only the right to own and use guns for the common, or collective, defense of society through a militia composed of citizens. They say that the Constitution does not protect the individual citizen's right to own and use weapons. Therefore, they say, government can limit and even prohibit guns.

People on both sides of the gun control debate engage in an activity called lobbying. When they lobby, they try to influence lawmakers to vote in favor of their particular viewpoints.

Individual Right

The individual right view is accepted by only a minority of legal experts. But it is accepted by a vocal part of the American general public. This part of the public lobbies heavily. Polls show that the "pro-gun" lobby represents a minority opinion in the United States. However, membership in pro-gun lobbying organizations far outnumbers that of the collective right organizations.

The National Rifle Association (NRA) is by far the largest and most powerful holder of the individual right view. Founded in 1871, it has a membership of about 3 million Americans. Its members are often called upon to send letters and telegrams opposing gun control to their elected officials.

According to the NRA, one of its main purposes is to "protect and defend the Constitution of the United States, especially with reference to the inalienable [not able to be taken away] right of the individual American citizen guaranteed by such Constitution to acquire, possess, transport, carry, transfer ownership of, and enjoy the right to use arms." This is a clear statement of the NRA's individual right view.

Collective Right

It was not until the twentieth century that the idea developed that the Second Amendment might protect a collective right to bear arms. Until the social unrest and string of assassinations in the 1960s, most people assumed that the amendment guaranteed to individual citizens the right to possess and use arms without restriction. That violent period of U.S. history, however, led many people to consider a different interpretation of the Second Amendment's meaning.

The collective right view has come to be widely held by lawyers and law professors. The view has been upheld by most courts that have dealt in recent years with the issues surrounding the Second Amendment. In the words of the American Civil Liberties Union

(ACLU), an organization that traditionally defends individual rights, "The setting in which the Second Amendment was proposed and adopted demonstrates that the right to bear arms is a collective one, existing only in the collective population of each state for the purpose of maintaining an effective state militia."

The collective right supporters have formed their own lobby, the "gun control" lobby. Handgun Control, Inc., is the largest organization in the gun control lobby, with a membership of about 1 million Americans. One of its spokespeople is Sarah Brady, the wife of James Brady. He was the presidential press secretary who was shot in an assassination attempt on Ronald Reagan in 1981.

Supporters of both the individual right and collective right views base their very different interpretations of the Second Amendment on several arguments. They argue over these things: the wording of the Second Amendment, the history of the amendment, the intentions of the Framers of the Bill of Rights, and the decisions of the U.S. Supreme Court relating to the Second Amendment.

The Wording of the Second Amendment

Many of the words used in the Second Amendment can be defined in different ways. Some of the commonly accepted meanings of the words chosen by the Framers of the Amendment have changed since the Bill of Rights was drafted. The words discussed by both sides in the gun control debate include *militia, people,* and *bear.*

The individual right view uses the broadest definition of the word *militia.* In eighteenth-century English one definition of *militia* included the entire able-bodied adult male population. According to this definition (updated for the twentieth century to include the adult male and female population), almost everyone is in the militia. And, say the supporters of the individual right view, everyone in the militia has the right to keep and bear arms.

The collective right view, on the other hand, uses a more narrow definition of the word *militia.* Today a *militia* is most commonly defined as an army composed of trained citizens rather than

"...The Right Of The People To Keep And Bear Arms..." — *Second Amendment, U.S. Constitution*

REUTERS/BETTMANN NEWSPHOTOS: JUNE 3 - An unidentified demonstrator beaten by troops near Beijing's Great Hall of the People on Saturday manages to stagger away from his assailants.

Today's Headlines Remind Us Why.

The students of Beijing did not have a Second Amendment right to defend themselves when the soldiers came. All they had was the hope and dream of liberty. Because tyranny cannot tolerate armed citizens, these brave young Chinese could only hurl words and hold out empty hands against an army.

There is no right to bear arms in Soviet Georgia. Once again, a totalitarian regime would not tolerate it. That's why the Georgian people could not stop Soviet agents from first registering and later confiscating 66,000 personal firearms. Dictators are quick to send their soldiers against speechmakers. But not against armed citizens.

America's founding fathers understood that an armed people are a free people. Free to defend themselves against crime and violence. Free to rise up against tyranny. That's why the individual armed citizen remains one of democracy's strongest symbols.

The National Rifle Association's defense of firearms isn't just about hunting, or competitive shooting, or even personal protection. The right to own a firearm is a statement about freedom. If you don't get the message, take another look at the photographs. Read the headlines again. These words and images — and a million bitter tears — tell it all.

Paid for by the members of the National Rifle Association of America. ©1989

A National Rifle Association advertisement.

professional soldiers. Using this definition, one may understand the Second Amendment to give only a select group of militia members, not the whole country's population, the right to bear arms.

What did the Framers of the Bill of Rights mean by "the right of the people"? Supporters of the individual right view argue that the Second Amendment uses the phrase "the people" to include all the individual people in the country. The collective right supporters, on the other hand, believe that "the people" means the states. The First, Fourth, and Ninth Amendments also included this phrase. It is commonly accepted in these cases that "the right of the people" means individual rights, not necessarily the rights of a community or society.

The third word whose meaning is debated is *bear*. The individual right supporters argue that the phrase "to bear arms" has a military meaning. According to this viewpoint, individual citizens do not "bear" arms; instead, they "carry" or "use" them. Only soldiers "bear" arms. If the Framers had wanted only to protect the state militias, goes their argument, they would not have needed to include both the right to "keep" and the right to "bear" arms. A right to "bear" arms would have been enough to allow militia members to carry out their duties against attack, regardless of where their weapons were kept when they were off duty. The Framers, by also including the right to "keep" arms, wanted citizens to have easy access to their weapons at all times.

The Second Amendment's History

When the Second Amendment was being written, there was little difference between the individual and collective rights so strongly argued today. Militias were the most important defense. Today they are not. Private citizens were the soldiers. Today they are not. Privately owned guns were the weapons of war. Today they are not. People today are living in a very different time. Nevertheless, both sides of the gun control debate try to understand the historical period in which the Second Amendment was written.

A Handgun Control, Inc., advertisement.

Supporters of the collective right view argue that, at the time of the writing of the Bill of Rights, there was no police force for protection. Colonists relied on the local militia. Since then the standing U.S. Army, the National Guard, and state and local police forces have developed. Thus supporters of the collective right view argue that the idea of a state militia is outdated. As the militia has lost its importance to the U.S. government over the last century, there is no need for militia members to have the right to keep and bear guns.

Supporters of the individual right position remember the colonists' distrust of government. Armed citizens, they say, are a necessary part of the checks and balances wanted by the Founding Fathers. The militia was included in the Constitution as a check on the federal government, to prevent it from becoming dictatorial. Citizens were to be armed so they could protect their own rights and freedoms. Even today, the individual right supporters fear that the government might take away their guns and leave them defenseless against further limitations of their rights and freedoms.

The Founding Fathers' Ideas

A large part of the debate over the Second Amendment and gun control centers on interpreting the ideas of the Founding Fathers. Supporters of the individual right view argue that the Founding Fathers all owned firearms and praised individual ownership of guns. They state that George Washington owned fifty guns himself. They quote Thomas Jefferson: "One loves to possess arms." Their opinion is that individual ownership and use of guns was an assumed right. They support this opinion with the fact that the "right to bear arms" clause of the Second Amendment was one of the few clauses in the Bill of Rights not to be questioned and criticized during ratification.

The collective right view holds that when the Framers wrote and discussed the Second Amendment they were concerned only with protecting an organized militia. They point to the phrase that was originally included in the amendment: "but no person religiously scrupulous of bearing arms shall be compelled to render military service in person." According to the supporters of the collective right view, this phrase shows that the Framers were thinking of the Second Amendment as protection of the rights of members of state militias, not as protection of any individual right.

U.S. Supreme Court Decisions

The case of *United States* v. *Miller* (1939) is the only U.S. Supreme Court case ever to rule directly on the meaning of the Second Amendment. So it is often referred to by both the collective right and the individual right supporters.

Opponents of gun control look at specific types of weapons. The Supreme Court's decision in the *Miller* case (1939) implied that the more suitable any given weapon was for militia use, the less that weapon would be subject to congressional control. In other words weapons useful to a militia could be possessed by individual citizens. In fact, to some opponents of gun control, the *Miller* case has meant that an individual citizen has a right to keep and bear bazookas [weapons that launch armor-piercing rockets], rocket launchers, assault weapons, and all other arms that are clearly related to modern warfare.

Supporters of gun control laws have a different interpretation of the decision in the *Miller* case. The ACLU

agrees with the Supreme Court's long-standing interpretation of the Second Amendment as set forth in the 1939 case, *U.S.* v. *Miller:* that the right to bear arms applies only to the preservation of a well-regulated militia. Except for police and military purposes, we believe that the possession of weapons by individuals is not constitutionally protected. . . . [W]e believe that there is no constitutional objection to gun control laws in general.

Many hunters do not want the government regulating guns.

In other words, a restriction on the possession of weapons would only violate the Second Amendment if it prevented the efficient functioning of the militia. The state militias have been replaced by a National Guard whose weapons are provided by the federal government. So individual citizens no longer need to bear arms.

Effects on the Law of the Gun Control Lobby

Both the pro-gun lobby and the gun control lobby work hard to influence legislation at the state and national level. During the 1980 elections organizations opposing gun control—the pro-gun lobby—spent over $2 million for candidates supporting their views. Gun control groups spent less than one-tenth of that amount.

There are many local election campaigns that have turned into political battles between the NRA and gun control supporters. For example, in November 1982, California voters were deciding on a referendum (a law given to the general public to vote upon) called Proposition 15. The proposed law provided for a limit on privately held handguns. It required all handgun owners to register their weapons. It was a great opportunity for both sides in the gun control debate to try to convince the California public of their views on the Second Amendment.

The collective right groups spent just over $2 million on advertising and publicity in the California campaign. The individual right groups spent more than $6 million. Californians rejected the proposal to require gun registration by more than 2 to 1.

In 1988 the NRA spent $2 million to successfully block relatively mild congressional gun restrictions. In that same year the NRA spent $6 million in an attempt to stop passage of a Maryland ban on Saturday night specials. While it spent more money than was ever before spent for any campaign in the state (more even than for the governor's campaign), the NRA failed to stop the law. It is obvious that many Americans are willing to pay money to see their interpretation of the Second Amendment become law.

There is no easy answer to the gun control debate. Both sides have good arguments that come from their interpretation of the Second Amendment. Both sides will continue to spend large amounts of money trying to convince people that their interpretation is right. In the end Americans must decide for themselves what the Second Amendment really means.

CHAPTER 7

The Second Amendment: What Does It Mean Today?

"The right of citizens to bear arms is just one more guarantee against arbitrary government, one more safeguard against the tyranny which now appears remote in America, but which historically has proved to be always possible."

former U.S. Vice President HUBERT HUMPHREY

"[O]ur complex society requires a rethinking of the proper role of firearms in modern America. Our forefathers used firearms as an integral part of their struggle for survival. But today firearms are not appropriate for daily life in the United States."

SENATOR EDWARD KENNEDY

From the 1960s until the present, the Second Amendment has become the center of more attention and interpretation than ever before. It is often the subject of editorials and letters to the editor in major newspapers. It has been examined in articles in legal journals. It has been studied by supporters and opponents of gun control. Many cases seeking to define its meaning have reached the lower courts.

The Right to Bear Arms: The Situation Around the World

Roughly one-half of the homes in the United States have at least one gun in them. An estimated 70 million Americans own 140 million rifles and 60 million handguns. Americans own about 3

A family at an outdoor rifle range in Arizona. Teaching teenagers to use guns is a controversial issue for many parents.

million semiautomatic weapons. These are especially large numbers for a country with secure borders, a nuclear defense system, and an armed police force. The mass production of firearms in this country and the glamorous portrayal of guns on television have helped guns to remain such an important part of American life even after many of their traditional uses have disappeared. Whether or not it was intended to do so, the Second Amendment has also helped guns to remain an important part of American life.

In almost no other part of the world are civilians as free to own and use guns as they are in the United States. The United States is the only modern urban industrial nation that still has such a close tie to guns in its culture. It is the only industrial nation where the possession of rifles, shotguns, and handguns is legal and widespread among large numbers of people.

The situation in Great Britain has always been closely watched and compared to the situation in the United States. The sale and possession of guns have been tightly regulated in Britain since the first gun control laws were passed there in the 1920s. Today, there are 840,000 registered shotguns and probably fewer rifles and handguns (since shotgun sports are the most popular in Britain). And the traditional militia has been completely replaced by unarmed police officers called "Bobbies."

In Canada there has been some form of handgun control for almost 100 years. Canadians do not have easy access to firearms. In 1978 new federal legislation required strict gun registration. The president of the Shooting Federation of Canada (the closest thing Canada has to the National Rifle Association [NRA] in the United States) explained, "There are vast cultural differences between Canada and the United States. We didn't have their tradition of a violent revolution to overthrow the oppressors, the Motherland. As well, we didn't have that seeming lawlessness of the American West."

In Switzerland, on the other hand, almost every home has a gun. Switzerland relies on its militia instead of having regular armed forces. Under the militia system almost every adult male is legally required to possess a gun. Enlisted men are given automatic assault rifles by the government, and officers are given pistols. In a nation of 6 million people, there are at least 2 million guns, including 600,000 fully automatic assault rifles, half a million pistols, and numerous machine guns. Switzerland is one of the few nations having a higher rate of gun ownership than the United States.

Current State of the Laws

It is estimated that there are some 22,000 gun control laws in the various local, state, and federal jurisdictions in the United States. Forty-three states have "right to bear arms" provisions in their constitutions. Most states have laws that prohibit people from carrying concealed weapons and require them to get a permit or registration before they can own or use at least some types of guns. In fact every state except Vermont prohibits at least the carrying of a concealed handgun off one's own property. Texas and several other states absolutely prohibit the carrying of pistols by private individuals.

Some cities, like Chicago, New York, and Washington, D.C., have strict regulations on the sale and possession of handguns. But these regulations do not work well, because handguns can be easily gotten in neighboring areas and brought back to the cities.

The U.S. Congress in 1986 passed the Firearms Owners Protection Act. Called the "most historic piece of pro-gun legislation ever enacted" by the NRA, this law repealed many parts of the Gun Control Act of 1968. It allows interstate sales of rifles and shotguns. It permits interstate transportation of personally owned firearms that are unloaded and carefully secured. Thus it overrides local and state laws restricting or banning such transportation. Also passed in 1986 was a federal law prohibiting the manufacture and sale of new machine guns for civilians. The NRA asked the U.S. Supreme Court to rule on the constitutionality of this law. In 1991 the Court decided not to hear the case. The law therefore remains in effect.

Several recently proposed federal laws have dealt specifically with the sale of handguns. In 1988 President Reagan signed a federal law preventing the sale of plastic, undetectable handguns.

Each year for the last several years, Congress has voted on the so-called Brady bill, named after Sarah Brady, the wife of former President Reagan's press secretary, James Brady. The Brady bill proposes a seven-day "waiting period" for handgun buyers. Facing strong opposition from the NRA, it has been defeated each time it has been introduced. It was defeated most recently in the fall of 1990, when it did not come up for a congressional vote.

In 1988 a man named Patrick Purdy used an assault-style gun called an AK-47 to shoot thirty children and one teacher on a school playground in Stockton, California. Five children died. Purdy's attack was the fifth attack on schoolchildren in the year.

Congress responded in July 1989 with a law banning imports of military assault-style weapons. This type of weapon was not thought to be suitable for use in sports or hunting. The law prohibited the importation of forty-three types of foreign-made weapons and did not affect the sale of assault-style weapons made in the United States.

In 1990, however, the governmental office that handles gun restrictions, the U.S. Bureau of Alcohol, Tobacco, and Firearms, decided to allow some of the banned weapons to once again enter the United States. Since the 1989 law was passed, the weapons had been slightly changed by foreign manufacturers to fit the new restrictions.

Does the U.S. Need an Armed Citizenry?

International events have added fuel to the fire of argument surrounding the Second Amendment. The violent government repression of unarmed Chinese university students at Tiananmen Square in May 1989 led many people to argue against the government's prohibition of ownership of arms.

Writing about why such repression could not happen in the United States, American newspapers quickly pointed to the protection of the right to keep and bear arms by the Second Amendment:

"[I]f all Chinese citizens kept arms, their rulers would hardly have dared to massacre the demonstrators. . . ." Just after the Tiananmen Square massacre, a letter to the editor of the *New York Times* asked, "Who knows what the leaders and the military and the police of our America will be up to at some point in the future? We need an armed citizenry to protect our liberty."

Others argue that even armed U.S. citizens would not be able to protect their liberty against a better-armed government. A 1989 article in a law school journal asked: "Of what serious value are handguns or even machine guns against the arsenal of the modern state? For that matter, of what serious assistance are handguns and machine guns for the *defense* of the state in a nuclear age?"

Sylvester Stallone starred in a number of Rambo films in which the use of firearms in violent situations proved a popular box office attraction.

In the 1980s and 1990s, rising crime rates were met with demands for gun control laws and with the purchase of guns for self-protection.

Public Opinion in the United States

A majority of the American people supports the right of law-abiding citizens to own firearms for self-defense and sporting purposes. A majority also supports laws that would help keep firearms out of the hands of criminals and mentally ill people. U.S.

citizens generally believe that while guns can and should be controlled and regulated, they should not be prohibited. Guns may be needed for self-defense.

A 1975 public opinion survey found that 78 percent of the U.S. population believed that the U.S. Constitution gave them the right to keep and bear arms. When asked whether the "right to keep and bear arms" applied to the individual citizen or only to the National Guard, 78 percent said the individual citizen.

A 1990 poll reported that 87 percent of gun owners themselves supported a seven-day waiting period for handgun purchases (like that proposed to Congress in the Brady bill). Three-quarters support registration of semiautomatic weapons and handguns. Half support registration of rifles and shotguns.

Public opinion in the United States is heavily affected by crime coverage in newspapers and television. In 1990 much attention was focused on the Second Amendment when a rash of shootings of children in New York City was heavily covered by the media. In two weeks during the summer, six young children were shot by stray bullets or guns in the hands of other children.

In response to the shootings, public calls for gun control grew louder. Newspapers wrote strong editorials in support of gun laws. One encouraged the U.S. Congress to

> take the highly effective step of providing a seven-day waiting period between the purchase of a handgun and the possession of it. In the interim, police would run background checks on the buyer. If he or she were a felon, a fugitive, an alcohol or drug abuser, or had been judged mentally incompetent in court, Federal law would prohibit ownership of the weapon. No sportsman or home defender would suffer; no constitutional right, however disputed, would be violated.

Only time will tell if this recent round of shootings will lead to another round of gun control laws.

CHAPTER 8

The Future of the Second Amendment

"How much more horrifying can the evidence get, before it becomes clear to all that guns. . . . are too easily obtained, kept and used in this country, by almost anyone?"

TOM WICKER, *New York Times*

"To 'keep and bear arms' for hunting today is . . . not an imperative of survival, as it was 200 years ago; 'Saturday night specials' and machine guns are not recreational weapons and surely are as much in need of regulation as motor vehicles."

WARREN E. BURGER, former Chief Justice of the United States

In the fall of 1990, the U.S. Congress worked to pass a new anticrime law. One of its measures would have banned for three years the import, making, sale, and possession of nine kinds of semiautomatic weapons. The types of guns that would have been banned are not used by hunters, but by street criminals and drug traffickers. The law passed the Senate in July 1990. But in the final days of the congressional session, the ban on semiautomatic weapons was removed from the law to make it more acceptable. The weaker law was then approved by the House of Representatives.

Also under congressional consideration was the so-called Brady bill, which would have required a seven-day waiting period for the

---

According to Supreme Court rulings, the right to bear arms is one of the few sections of the Bill of Rights that still does not protect citizens against state and local actions to curtail that right.

purchase of a handgun. Although it had over 150 cosponsors or supporters in the House of Representatives, a vote was not taken on the bill.

Despite their failure in Congress, there seemed to be enough public support for both of these bills. It has been suggested that their failure was due to strong lobbying by the National Rifle Association (NRA). A future session of Congress may be more able to resist such lobbying efforts. It may be the case in the future that the private ownership and use of at least some assault-style weapons will be illegal in the United States. U.S. citizens may have to wait a week to purchase a handgun. The right of individual citizens to keep and bear guns will have been further limited by federal law.

As crime rates continue to rise in the United States, Americans may be willing to give up any individual right they may have to keep and bear arms in order to make it harder for criminals to get guns. On the other hand, Americans may demand the individual right to bear arms to protect themselves from such criminals.

It is not at all likely that either the federal or state governments will try to completely ban the sale or possession of all firearms. It is possible that the sale or possession of some types of weapons that are not generally used for military or police purposes may be prohibited by federal law. For example, the Saturday night special will not likely be adopted for military or police use. A strong case can be made that the people's right to own and use a Saturday night special is not protected under the Second Amendment. It may eventually be federally banned. In the words of retired Chief Justice Warren Burger, " 'Saturday night specials' and machine guns are not recreational weapons and surely are as much in need of regulation as motor vehicles."

There are other kinds of dangerous weapons: brass knuckles (linked metal rings or a metal bar with holes for the fingers), blackjacks (leather-covered clubs with flexible handles), sandbags (small, narrow bags of sand used as clubs), switchblade knives, and sawed-off shotguns. All of these weapons would probably not be

Both supporters and opponents of gun control interpret the Second Amendment in ways that support their own position.

used by a militia or National Guard unit. All may eventually be banned as well. Also, any arms that are too big or heavy for an individual citizen to "keep and bear" may be outlawed.

It is also possible that future national legislation will prohibit the possession of long guns—those with long barrels, such as rifles and shotguns—by city dwellers. There are several unacceptably dangerous side effects of firing such weapons in urban areas. Their bullets go much farther through people and walls, increasing the risk of wounding innocent people. The spray of ammunition by automatic weapons is also more likely to hit others than the intended target. The risk of accidental firing is greater with long guns than with handguns. Long guns are harder to hide from curious children who may accidentally fire them.

It may become federal law that the open carrying of handguns is prohibited unless a permit is obtained first. Limited exceptions to this law might include the carrying of handguns for target shooting or transporting to a repair shop.

All of these potential laws would directly affect the current meaning of the Second Amendment. Most, if not all, would be challenged in the courts. While the U.S. Supreme Court has discussed some aspects of the Second Amendment, it has not ruled clearly and directly on whether the amendment guarantees an individual right to bear arms or a collective right to armed defense.

Eventually, the Supreme Court might be called upon to hear a case that will require a decision on this aspect of the meaning of the Second Amendment. If this happens—and if the Court decides to rule on it—the case will be very closely watched by both supporters and opponents of gun control laws, as well as by students and teachers of constitutional law. The outcome of such a case will go far in deciding what rights the Second Amendment should protect. Nevertheless, unless the Supreme Court rules that the Second Amendment applies not just to the federal government but also to the state governments, such a ruling may not affect most people.

It is possible to imagine that, in the future, a new constitutional amendment might be proposed and ratified. Such an amendment might change the meaning of, or completely reverse, the Second Amendment.

Whatever happens, the U.S. Congress, the U.S. Supreme Court, and the American public would do well to remember the Framers of the Bill of Rights. They worked hard to create a Bill of Rights, and specifically a Second Amendment, that would be in the best interest of this nation. In the Second Amendment, they protected a right that they considered to be fundamental to freedom. As the United States prepares to enter the twenty-first century, the freedoms protected by the Bill of Rights are just as fundamental as they were over two hundred years ago.

$\mathscr{I}$MPORTANT $\mathscr{D}$ATES

1689 English Bill of Rights protests King James II's use of a standing army.

1770 Tension around presence of British army in Boston leads to Boston Massacre.

1776 Declaration of Independence is proclaimed (announced) as a protest against British colonial rule.

1776 Virginia is first state to adopt its own Declaration of Rights, including a provision for an armed militia.

1786– Shays's Rebellion challenges local militias in Massachusetts and shows
1787 weakness of government under Articles of Confederation.

1787 U.S. Constitution is written by delegates to the Constitutional Convention meeting in Philadelphia.

1789 Before U.S. House of Representatives, James Madison proposes a series of changes to the U.S. Constitution.

1791 U.S. Bill of Rights, including Second Amendment, becomes law.

1792 U.S. Congress passes the first Militia Act, which requires white men to enroll in their state militias.

1812 Unreliable performance of state militias in War of 1812 shows uncertainty of their use for U.S. defense.

1813 Kentucky becomes first state to pass a law outlawing the carrying of concealed weapons.

1822 In *Bliss* v. *Commonwealth,* Kentucky court overturns 1813 ban on the carrying of concealed weapons.

1835 Native Americans begin forced moves to reservations farther west; United States provides those who move with guns and other supplies.

1849 Congress begins to give surplus army weapons to settlers moving west.

1862 A new Militia Act accepts African-American men into Union militias.

1865 After the end of the Civil War, Southern states adopt "black codes" that restrict gun usage by African Americans.

1866 U.S. Congress passes Civil Rights Act, which aims to protect African Americans' rights as U.S. citizens.

1866 To guarantee rights of U.S. citizenship, the Fourteenth Amendment to the U.S. Constitution is proposed.

1871 National Rifle Association is founded as an organization for hunters and sportsmen.

1876 U.S. Supreme Court decides in *United States* v. *Cruikshank* that the Second Amendment applies only to the federal government and not to the state governments.

1876 U.S. Congress bans sales of some types of ammunition to Native Americans.

1886 U.S. Supreme Court rules in *Presser* v. *Illinois* that states can limit the right to bear arms as long as an effective state militia is maintained.

1894 U.S. Supreme Court upholds a state law prohibiting the carrying of deadly weapons in *Miller* v. *Texas.*

1903 U.S. Congress passes a new Militia Act, placing state militias under authority of U.S. president and creating a national reserve force called the National Guard.

1911 New York state legislature passes the Sullivan Law, restricting the sale, possession, and use of deadly weapons.

1919 U.S. Congress passes War Revenues Act, placing first tax on sales of firearms.

1927 Miller bill to limit mail-order sales of concealable guns is passed by U.S. Congress and signed into law.

1934 U.S. Congress limits use of "gangster weapons" by passing National Firearms Act, first federal law to restrict keeping and bearing of firearms.

1938 U.S. Congress passes Federal Firearms Act, giving federal government more control over gun sales.

1939 U.S. Supreme Court upholds National Firearms Act of 1934 in *United States* v. *Miller.*

1942 *Cases* v. *United States* is heard by a U.S. Court of Appeals, which decides that the federal government can limit the right to keep and bear firearms but cannot prohibit any weapon that could be used by a person serving in a militia.

1963 President John F. Kennedy is assassinated with a mail-order rifle while riding in a motorcade in Texas.

1965 Muslim minister and African-American leader Malcolm X is assassinated in New York City.

1968 Civil rights leader Dr. Martin Luther King, Jr., is assassinated with a rifle on the balcony of his motel room in Memphis, Tennessee.

1968 Gun Control Act is passed by U.S. Congress in an attempt to control gun-related violence.

1975 President Gerald R. Ford survives two assassination attempts in one month.

1976 A U.S. Court of Appeals hears *United States* v. *Warin,* ruling that congressional regulation of firearms is constitutional.

1977 U.S. Supreme Court decides in *Lewis* v. *United States* to allow prevention of certain groups of people from having or using any firearm.

1979 Last restrictions on Native American gun ownership are lifted.

1981 President Ronald Reagan and his press secretary James Brady survive an assassination attempt that uses a Saturday night special.

1981 Handgun Crime Control Act, which includes a seven-day waiting period for the purchase of a handgun, is introduced for the first time in U.S. Congress but fails to pass.

1981 Town of Morton Grove, Illinois, bans the sale or possession of handguns within its limits.

1982 Californians reject gun registration by voting down Proposition 15, a law that would have required all handgun owners to register their firearms.

1986 U.S. Congress passes Firearms Owners Protection Act, repealing parts of 1968 Gun Control Act by allowing interstate sales and transportation of firearms.

1986 U.S. Congress bans sale and manufacture of new machine guns for civilians.

1988 U.S. Congress passes federal law banning plastic, undetectable guns.

1988 Voters in Maryland choose to ban Saturday night specials, despite heavy pressure from National Rifle Association against the ban.

1989 In response to a schoolyard attack with an AK-47 in California, U.S. Congress bans import of forty-three types of military assault-style weapons.

1990 U.S. Bureau of Alcohol, Tobacco, and Firearms allows import of some previously banned assault-style weapons.

GLOSSARY

amendment   A change in the Constitution.

appeal   To refer a case to a higher court to review the decision of a lower court.

assize   An ancient kind of court made up of knights and other important people, with a baron of justice, which met at a certain place at an appointed time. They were summoned together to try a disputed cause, performing the functions of a jury, except that they gave a verdict based on their own investigation and knowledge, not from evidence presented. It developed into an English superior court for the trial of civil and criminal cases in most counties by judges traveling on circuit.

bail   Money paid by the accused to gain his or her release in the period before trial to make sure he or she will show up for the trial. If the accused does not, he or she loses the money.

bill of attainder   A law pronouncing a person guilty of a serious crime without a trial.

dissenting opinion   An opinion by one or more of a court's judges that disagrees with a majority opinion.

double jeopardy   The putting of a person on trial for a crime for which he or she has already been put on trial.

executive branch   The branch or part of the government that carries the laws into effect and makes sure they are obeyed.

ex post facto **laws**   Laws that make illegal those actions that took place before the passage of the law.

federalism   The relationships between the states and the federal government, each having certain special powers and sharing others.

immunity   Freedom from penalties and duties.

incorporation   The process of making the rights in the Bill of Rights apply to the states so that people are guaranteed to be safeguarded against state actions that might violate their rights. The Fourteenth Amendment's due process clause is used as the basis for this process.

indictment   A grand jury's written accusation naming the person charged with a crime and charging that person with the crime.

judicial branch   The part or branch of the government that interprets the laws and settles disputes under the law.

judicial review   The power of the courts to review the decisions of other parts or levels of the government. Courts may review the decisions of lower courts and come to a different decision.

legislative branch   The part or branch of the government that makes the laws.

majority opinion   The statement of the decision of a court in which the majority of its members join.

militia   The body of citizens of a state, enrolled for participation as a military force, but not engaged in actual service except in emergencies, in contrast to regular troops or a standing army.

musket   A heavy, large-caliber usually muzzle-loading shoulder firearm with a smooth bore.

ratification   Approval of an amendment by three-fourths of state legislatures or conventions (after the amendment has been officially proposed by two-thirds of each house of Congress or proposed by a convention called by two-thirds of the states).

rifle   A shoulder weapon with spiral groove in its bore.

Saturday night special   A cheap easily concealed handgun.

separation of powers   The division of the government into three parts or branches—the legislative, the executive, and the judicial.

standing army   A permanent army of paid soldiers.

$\mathscr{S}$UGGESTED $\mathscr{R}$EADING

Abrams, Daniel. "The 'Right' to Bear Arms in America." *USA Today*, vol. 118, no. 2540, May 1990, pp. 22–23.

Bakal, Carl. *The Right to Bear Arms.* New York: McGraw-Hill Book Co., 1966.

The Bill of Rights and Beyond: A Resource Guide. The Commission on the Bicentennial of the United States Constitution, 1990.

Brant, Irving. *The Bill of Rights: Its Origin and Meaning.* New York: The Bobbs-Merrill Company, Inc., 1965.

*Center to Prevent Handgun Violence. *Guns and the Constitution: The Debate over the Second Amendment.* Washington, D.C.: Center to Prevent Handgun Violence, 1987.

*Colman, Warren. *The Bill of Rights.* Chicago: Childrens Press, 1987.

Congressional Research Service. *The Constitution of the United States of America: Analysis and Interpretation.* Washington, D.C.: U.S. Government Printing Office, 1987.

*Cress, Lawrence Delbert. "The Founding Fathers and the Right to Bear Arms: A Well-Regulated Militia." *this Constitution,* no. 14 (Spring 1987), pp. 21–23.

Dumbauld, Edward. *The Bill of Rights and What It Means Today.* Norman: University of Oklahoma Press, 1957.

Jordan, Philip D. "The Wearing of Weapons in the Western Country." In *Frontier Law and Order: Ten Essays.* Lincoln: University of Nebraska Press, 1970, pp. 1–22.

Kates, Don B., ed. *Restricting Handguns: The Liberal Skeptics Speak Out.* Croton-on-Hudson: North River Press, Inc., 1979.

*Katz, William Loren, and Bernard Gaughran. *The Constitutional Amendments.* New York: Franklin Watts, Inc., 1974.

Kelly, Alfred H., Winfred A. Harbison, and Herman Belz. *The American Constitution: Its Origins and Development.* 6th ed. New York: W.W. Norton & Co., 1983.

*Lindop, Edmund. *Birth of the Constitution.* Hillside, N.J.: Enslow Publishers, Inc., 1987.

Rutland, Robert Allen. *The Birth of the Bill of Rights.* Chapel Hill: University of North Carolina Press, 1955.

Schwartz, Bernard. *The Great Rights of Mankind: A History of the Bill of Rights.* New York: Oxford University Press, 1977.

*Shalhope, Robert E. "The Founding Fathers and the Right to Bear Arms: To Keep the People Duly Armed." *this Constitution,* no. 14 (Spring 1987), pp. 18–20.

U.S. Senate. *The Right to Keep and Bear Arms: Report of the Subcommittee on the Constitution of the Committee on the Judiciary.* Washington, D.C.: U.S. Government Printing Office, 1982.

*Readers of *The Second Amendment* by Joan C. Hawxhurst may find this book particularly readable.

OURCES

American Civil Liberties Union. "Policy #47: Gun Control." In *ACLU Policy Guide*. As adopted at June 14–15, 1980 national board meeting. Mimeograph. ACLU office, New York City, pp. 95–96.

American Enterprise Institute for Public Policy Research. *Gun Control: Legislative Analysis No. 9, 94th Congress*. Washington, D.C.: American Enterprise Institute for Public Policy Research, 1976.

Anderson, Jervis. *Guns in American Life*. New York: Random House, 1984.

Bilski, Andrew. "Arms and the States: Gun Control is a Shared Concern." *Macleans*, July 3, 1989, pp. 36–37.

Black, William A. "Citizens Without Guns." *New York Times*, June 18, 1989.

Boorstin, Daniel J. *The Americans: The Colonial Experience*. New York: Random House, 1958.

Brown, Wendy. "Guns, Cowboys, Philadelphia Mayors, and Civic Republicanism: On Sanford Levinson's *The Embarrassing Second Amendment.*" *The Yale Law Journal* 99, no. 3 (December 1989), pp. 661–667.

Burger, Warren E. "The Right to Bear Arms." *Parade,* January 14, 1990, pp. 4–6.

Cassidy, J. Warren. "Here We Stand." *American Rifleman* 137, no. 8 (August 1989), p. 7.

Cress, Lawrence Delbert. "An Armed Community: The Origins and Meaning of the Right to Bear Arms." *The Journal of American History* 71, no. 1 (June 1984), pp. 22–42.

Emery, Lucilius A. "The Constitutional Right to Keep and Bear Arms." *Harvard Law Review* 28, no. 5 (March 1915), pp. 473–477.

Feller, Peter Buck, and Karl L. Gotting. "The Second Amendment: A Second Look." *Northwestern University Law Review* 61 (March–April 1966), pp. 46–70.

Fraenkel, Osmond K. *Our Civil Liberties*. New York: The Viking Press, 1944.

Gottlieb, Alan M. "Gun Ownership: A Constitutional Right." *Northern Kentucky Law Review* 10, no. 1 (1982), pp. 113–140.

Halbrook, Stephen P. *That Every Man Be Armed: The Evolution of a Constitutional Right*. Albuquerque: University of New Mexico Press, 1984.

Kates, Don B., Jr. "Handgun Prohibition and the Original Meaning of the Second Amendment." *Michigan Law Review* 82, no. 2 (November 1983), pp. 204–273.

Kennedy, Edward M. "The Handgun Crime Control Act of 1981." *Northern Kentucky Law Review* 10, no. 1 (1982), pp. 1–11.

Kennett, Lee, and James LaVerne Anderson. *The Gun in America: The Origins of a National Dilemma*. Westport, Conn.: Greenwood Press, 1975.

Knight, Harold V. *With Liberty and Justice for All: The Meaning of the Bill of Rights Today.* Dobbs Ferry, N.Y.: Oceana Publications, Inc., 1967.

Kukla, Robert K. *Gun Control.* Harrisburg, Penn.: Stackpole Books, 1973.

Levin, John. "The Right to Bear Arms: The Development of the American Experience." *Chicago-Kent Law Review* 48 (1971), pp. 148–167.

Levinson, Sanford. "The Embarrassing Second Amendment." *The Yale Law Journal* 99, no. 3 (December 1989), pp. 637–659.

Levy, Leonard W. *Encyclopedia of the American Constitution.* New York: Macmillan Publishing Co., 1986.

Mann, James L., III. "The Right to Bear Arms." *South Carolina Law Review* 19 (1967), pp. 402–413.

McGee, James H. "Voting Power = Gun Rights!" *Guns & Ammo* 34, no. 5 (May 1990), pp. 32–34.

Millis, Walter. *The Constitution and the Common Defense.* New York: The Fund for the Republic, Inc., 1959.

Pierce, Darell R. "Second Amendment Survey." *Northern Kentucky Law Review* 10, no. 1 (1982), pp. 155–162.

Prucha, Francis Paul, ed. *Documents of United States Indian Policy.* Lincoln: University of Nebraska, 1990.

Rohner, Ralph J. "The Right to Bear Arms: A Phenomenon of Constitutional History." *Catholic University Law Review* 16 (1966), pp. 53–84.

Schwartz, Bernard. *The Bill of Rights: A Documentary History.* Vols. 1 and 2. New York: Chelsea House Publishers, 1971.

Shalhope, Robert E. "The Ideological Origins of the Second Amendment." *The Journal of American History* 69, no. 3 (December 1982), pp. 599–614.

Singletary, Otis A. *Negro Militia and Reconstruction.* Westport, Conn.: Greenwood Press, 1984.

Sprecher, Robert A. "The Lost Amendment." *ABA Journal* 51 (1965), pp. 554–557.

Washburn, Wilcomb E. *The American Indian and the United States: A Documentary History.* Vol. 1. New York: Random House, 1973.

Webster, David J. *Myth and the History of the Hispanic Southwest.* The Calvin P. Horn Lectures in Western History and Culture, University of New Mexico, November 8–11, 1987. Albuquerque: University of New Mexico Press, 1988.

White, R.J. *The Horizon Concise History of England.* New York: American Heritage Publishing Co., Inc., 1971.

Wicker, Tom. "The Guns of America." *New York Times,* August 2, 1990.

Wimmershoff-Caplan. "The Founders and the AK–47." *Washington Post,* July 6, 1989.

$\mathscr{I}$NDEX OF $\mathscr{C}$ASES

Photograph and Text Credits

Cover: Department of Defense; 2–3: Independence Hall National Park; 10: © Dean Brown/Omni-Photo Communications; 10 (inset): Colonial Williamsburg; 11 (top): © Brad Markel/Gamma-Liaison; 11 (bottom): © Dean Brown/Omni-Photo Communications; 12: R. Michael Stuckey/Comstock; 14: Colonial Williamsburg; 16: "Raising the Liberty Pole," by John McRae/Kennedy Galleries; 18–19: Independence Hall National Park; 28: The Granger Collection; 31: Laurie Platt Winfrey; 33 and 35: Scala/Art Resource; 37: The Mansell Collection; 44 and 47: The Granger Collection; 56: Washington University Gallery of Art, St. Louis, Gift of Nathaniel Phillips, Boston, 1890; 59: The Granger Collection; 62: Courtesy of the Amon Carter Museum, Fort Worth, Texas; 65: Library of Congress; 72: © Al Grillo/Picture Group; 76 and 79: UPI/Bettmann; 82: UPI/Bettmann Newsphotos; 86: Culver Pictures; 97: UPI/Bettmann Newsphotos; 99: UPI/Bettmann; 100: © 1983 Alon Reininger/Woodfin Camp & Associates; 101: National Rifle Association of America and Handgun Control, Inc.; 105: National Rifle Association of America and Reuters/Bettmann Newsphotos; 107: Handgun Control, Inc.; 110: UPI/Bettmann; 112: © Dan Budnik 1980/Woodfin Camp & Associates; 117: Kobal Collection/Superstock, Inc.; 118: © 1981 Gerald Davis/Woodfin Camp & Associates; 120: R. Michael Stuckey/Comstock; 123: © 1981/Alon Reininger/Woodfin Camp & Associates.

Joan C. Hawxhurst is a free-lance writer who lives in Boulder, Colorado. She studied international relations at Yale University before doing human rights work in Argentina and Washington, D.C. She has written for newspapers, human rights organizations, and religious magazines.

Warren E. Burger was Chief Justice of the United States from 1969 to 1986. Since 1985 he has served as chairman of the Commission on the Bicentennial of the United States Constitution. He is also chancellor of the College of William and Mary, Williamsburg, Virginia; chancellor emeritus of the Smithsonian Institution; and a life trustee of the National Geographic Society. Prior to his appointment to the Supreme Court, Chief Justice Burger was Assistant Attorney General of the United States (Civil Division) and judge of the United States Court of Appeals, District of Columbia Circuit.

Philip A. Klinkner graduated from Lake Forest College in 1985 and is now finishing his Ph.D. in political science at Yale University. He is currently a Governmental Studies Fellow at the Brookings Institution in Washington, D.C. Klinkner is the author of *The First Amendment* and *The Ninth Amendment* in *The American Heritage History of the Bill of Rights*.